CHOSEN WOMEN OF THE BIBLE

●

ETHEL L. HERR

L. 6

MOODY PRESS
CHICAGO

© 1976 by
THE MOODY BIBLE INSTITUTE
OF CHICAGO

Library of Congress Catalog
Card Number: 75-36503

ISBN: 0-8024-1297-1

The use of selected references from various versions of the Bible in this publication does not necessarily imply publisher endorsement of the versions in their entirety.

18 19 20 Printing/VP/Year 92 91 90 89 88 87

Contents

To my Mother,
one of God's extra special Chosen Women,
who has showed me what Christian womanhood
means in today's world.

Introduction

On a sunny May morning, my husband and I were traveling with our three children through the Italian Alps toward Venice. We had just passed through a charming village set down in a flat little valley.

At a sudden Y in the road, we stopped for a family consultation with the map. While my map-reading skills are famous for getting us lost, it is a rare occasion that my husband cannot find our bearings in a matter of minutes, once he has the map in hand.

But this was one of those occasions. So we debated and at length decided to go left. Shortly the narrow, winding road climbed through soft, green hills. Our view was one of the grandest of the day's trip: snowcapped peaks; medieval castles; broad, blossoming valleys.

However, except for a woman and her children gathering sticks for their fire, we shared the road with no one. We soon realized this route would never take us to Venice. So, descending the hill to the Y, we took the fork to the right and found our way without another detour.

One thing my many travels during military days taught me: on all sorts of roads, maps are a must. I carry one even in my home town. But they are often valueless without an interpreter.

Many women will never travel with their families to Venice, but all do travel the roadway of life. It, too, is often filled with obstacles, uncertainties, and enticingly dangerous side-roads. If we are to reach our destination in safety, we must have a good map.

God has provided just the map for us—the Bible. But when we consult it, why is it that it doesn't always clarify things? Could it be we need someone to help us interpret our map?

Several years ago I taught a Bible class of young mothers in my neighborhood. For most, it was their first serious encounter with the Scriptures. Using the following biographical studies, the class made the exciting discovery that the Bible is really practical!

They came to see it as their map for the road of life—beautifully laid out by the God who knows the way so well, effectively interpreted for women by one fascinating, feminine life after another.

As you trace the steps of these women through your Bible, the Lord will make them meaningful in your heart, your home, your world! No doubt you will agree that while God drew the map, His daughters help to point the way.

MAKING THE MOST OF YOUR STUDY

These studies are planned as a guide for individual or group Bible study. For maximum benefit in a group situation, each individual should work out the lessons ahead of time. Then, when you meet, you can compare notes and discuss the lesson together.

Here are some suggestions for private study:

1. *Pick a specific time and an undisturbed place for daily study.* A few minutes of unhurried study set apart faithfully each day will do more than several hours spent only occasionally.
2. *Gather the following tools:*
   a. *A Bible.* Which version you choose is not important. However, if you use the King James, I recommend you refer to at least one of the modern-language versions as a supplementary aid.
   b. *Notebook and pen or pencil.* Develop the habit of jotting down your questions, reactions, answers; you will remember them twice as long.
   c. *Set of clear Bible maps.* Usually found in the back of your Bible, they are also available in some encyclopedias, atlases, and Bible geography texts.
   d. *A good dictionary.* A Bible dictionary will also be helpful.
   e. *Supplementary reading.* In the bibliography at the end of each chapter are listed books which you will find

rewarding if you desire to dig deeper. Some of the books you may find in the public or church library near you. Others may be purchased from your Christian book supplier. A few are out of print but may still be in a library.

Caution! Do not let these books take the place of your study. They are for enrichment only!

3. *Study one Bible character at a time,* in the following way:
   a. *Pray.* Ask God to help you understand and learn something about Himself, yourself, your friends, your needs, your responsibilities.
   b. *Read the section, Introducing.* This brief character-sketch is usually a fictitious incident from the life of the woman, which presents her in her historical setting. It will help you project yourself into her time and feelings so that her experiences can speak to your present need.
   c. *Next, study the questions and explanatory notes, looking up the Scripture references.* Jot down your answers, questions, and impressions. Do the questions in order. If you have difficulty with one, go on to the next; you can come back to it or consult a friend or classmate.
   d. *List in your notebook the lessons you have learned for your life.* Make specific recommendations for resulting action you have to take in applying what you have learned. Ask God for strength and wisdom to carry out these actions.
   e. *Be sure to share something you learn with someone else.* Truth becomes clearer and more exciting as you share it.
4. *Finally, take time to enjoy yourself as you follow these immortal footprints.* Let them help you in the thrilling development of your own God-centered lifestyle.

SO YOU'RE LEADING THE BIBLE STUDY?

And you're scared to death?

Relax! It can be fun. Have you been asked to lead it every week? Or is it your turn next week, after which you will pass the honors on to Susy, next to you? In either case, don't panic—at least not before you have scanned these "seven simple secrets for successful study sessions":

1. *Be prepared.* Study the lesson a little harder than usual to get the jump on the rest of your class.
2. *Begin with a time of sharing and prayer.* Some women come with news or burdens they are bursting to share. They will be better class participants if you give them ten or fifteen minutes to unburden themselves first. If you do not feel confident to lead in prayer, that's no disgrace; just ask someone who does.
3. *Assign reading of introductions, questions, notes, and Scriptures by rotation.* Get everybody into the game. If your group is composed of several people who are new at looking up scripture references, or if time is short, do not insist on finding all the references. Italicized references in the lesson are usually supplementary and not absolutely essential to the understanding of the questions.
4. *Make use of the alphabetical index bookmark on page 9.* Make it clear that all women present are free to use it. If everyone uses it, newcomers will not feel conspicuous.
5. *Keep the discussion on the track* by doing *three things:*
   a. *Look for indications that someone wants to speak, but is hesitant.* Encourage 100 percent participation.
   b. *When the discussion begins to stray afield, remind your group of the intended goal of the lesson.* Suggest that those interested in pursuing the delectable side-roads do so later, on the telephone or over a cup of coffee.
   c. *When things get bogged down because a question seems unclear or a disagreement arises, go on to the next question.* Perhaps the problem will clear up as you progress.
6. *Never be embarrassed to admit your ignorance.* This study is designed to be a learning situation for the entire class—beginning with the leader!
7. *Remind class members to prepare next week's lesson before you meet again.*

Now, that's really not so hard, is it? Especially if you ask the Lord for strength as you tackle it.

Have a good class!

REFERENCE FINDER

Because many women are unfamiliar with their Bibles and experience awkwardness in finding references, the alphabetical index bookmark has been included below. Before beginning your study, look up the books in your own Bible, and jot down the page numbers on which they begin. Then clip the bookmark from this page, fold it on the dotted line (you may want to paste the sides together, as well), and keep it in your Bible or study book. Excellent help for future studies, too!

(cut)

(cut)

THE BOOKS OF THE BIBLE
IN ALPHABETICAL ORDER

Acts	_____	Jude	_____
Amos	_____	Judges	_____
Chronicles, 1	_____	Kings, 1	_____
Chronicles, 2	_____	Kings, 2	_____
Colossians	_____	Lamentations	_____
Corinthians, 1	_____	Leviticus	_____
Corinthians, 2	_____	Luke	_____
Daniel	_____	Malachi	_____
Deuteronomy	_____	Mark	_____
Ecclesiastes	_____	Matthew	_____
Ephesians	_____	Micah	_____
Esther	_____	Nahum	_____
Exodus	_____	Nehemiah	_____
Ezekiel	_____	Numbers	_____
Ezra	_____	Obadiah	_____
Galatians	_____	Peter, 1	_____
Genesis	_____	Peter, 2	_____
Habakkuk	_____	Philemon	_____
Haggai	_____	Philippians	_____
Hebrews	_____	Proverbs	_____
Hosea	_____	Psalms	_____
Isaiah	_____	Revelation	_____
James	_____	Romans	_____
Jeremiah	_____	Ruth	_____
Job	_____	Samuel, 1	_____
Joel	_____	Samuel, 2	_____
John	_____	Song of Solomon	_____
John, 1	_____	Thessalonians, 1	_____
John, 2	_____	Thessalonians, 2	_____
John, 3	_____	Timothy, 1	_____
Jonah	_____	Timothy, 2	_____
Joshua	_____	Titus	_____
		Zechariah	_____
		Zephaniah	_____

1
Eve

INTRODUCING EVE

Suppose you awaken to find yourself in a lush, green garden. It is filled with gorgeous birds and friendly beasts. All around you are trees heavily laden with tempting fruits. There are no supermarkets, no automobiles, no skyscrapers. In fact, there are no other people—just you and your husband!

Can you push your imagination a bit further? You have been alive only a few short hours!

With childlike fascination, you wander about your garden paradise. You breathe deeply and feel exhilarated by the pure air. You rub slender blades of grass between your fingers and examine fragrant, velvety flower petals. You toss tiny pebbles into clear pools of water and wonder at the operation of physical laws you can neither name nor understand.

You talk with the animals, stroking their fur, feeling their cold noses nudge against your leg. But as you walk hand in hand with your husband, you feel a special kinship with him. Though you sense differences between you, you know both of you are one and the same kind of being. With him, as with none of the animals, you can laugh and talk. Together you are learning, loving, playing, enjoying the many pleasures of your freshly created world.

In the cool evening hours, you and your husband talk with the God who created you. No, you do not see Him. But His strong, kind voice fills you with joy as each day He shares with you exciting new truths about life.

More than any other, one special secret about you alone perplexes and thrills you—that beautiful mystery of your unique earthly function of bearing children.

What is a child? How shall you care for it? How can it be formed in the hidden chambers of your body? You wonder, you question, you ponder!

Life is puzzling. You have no precedents to follow; no human patterns to copy; no refinements developed from childhood. No rivalries to fear, no triumphs to boast. No false guides to confuse. All you know about yourself and your responsibilities, you must learn from experience, your husband, and your loving God.

Oh yes, your names? God calls your husband *Adam*, meaning "human being." Adam, in turn, has named you *Eve*, "life giver"; for you are to become the mother of all human beings to come!

From you, all womankind will learn something about her place in an increasingly complex world. The precedents you establish will speak to your daughters throughout many centuries to come.

What an awesome place you hold! Yours are the first footprints to cross the turf of God's fresh, new earth.

WOMAN'S PLACE

We women live in a world of complex relationships that bless, challenge, and perplex us. In these studies we hope to see how different women's lives illustrate God's guidelines for ordering our relationships for the best possible good.

Eve's story demonstrates an ideal. It shows God's original design for our place in relation to (1) God, (2) men (especially our husbands), and (3) our children. It also explains what happened to mar that ideal and how God adapted the plan to fit the new, imperfect situation.

1. What was God's original intent in creating the world and, especially, human beings (Genesis 1:26-28; Psalm 8:6-8; Colossians 1:16)?

_____

_____

OBSERVATION: God is creative, and creativity must create. When He made man, God built into him, to a limited extent, this same creative capacity. Consider such areas as moral character, creative capacity, spiritual dimension.

2. In what ways do people reflect, as a mirror, "the image of God" mentioned in Genesis 1:26-27?

OBSERVATION: God also gave to man a free will. By choice he could yield himself to Satan and thus reflect the evils of satanic character through his life.

3. What was God's special purpose in creating woman (Genesis 1:28; 2:18)?

NOTE: The word "helpmeet" in the King James Version may be translated "suitable helper." Check other translations for further ideas.

OBSERVATION: God's created orders are superb. Wherever He has created a need, He has always provided the fulfillment of that need. Further, He has put in the needy creature a strong attraction to what he needs. To each creature He has given a different set of needs, so that all of creation is balanced.

For example, frogs need the specific nutrients found in insects. So God made insects to buzz around the ponds where frogs live. And He gave to frogs the strong urge to sit (on lily pads put there to aid the process!) and snap at flies and mosquitoes.

In man and woman we see this natural principle enacted at the highest level. We were made with important differences, to complement each other and with a strong attraction based largely on these differences. Hence, if we would experience life at its fullest, we must learn why the differences are there and how to use them for the maximum benefit.

4. According to Genesis 2:23-24, how are a man and his wife to be related to each other?

_____

_____

NOTE: "In the Lord, woman is not independent of man nor man independent of woman. For just as woman originates from man, so also man comes into existence through woman, but everything springs originally from God" (1 Corinthians 11:11-12, Weymouth[1]).

OBSERVATION: Matthew Henry, the great Bible commentator, suggested, "Woman was *made of a rib out of the side of Adam;* not made out of his head to rule over him, nor out of his feet to be trampled upon by him, but out of his side to be equal with him, under his arm to be protected, and near his heart to be beloved."[2]

5. Read the following verses from Proverbs. Note the high value placed on a good wife and the contrasting curse of a bad wife (Proverbs 12:4; 18:22; 19:13-14; 21:9, 19; 27:15-16; 31:10-31):

_____

_____

_____

OBSERVATION: One source of many marital problems is that the woman pursues her own interests so intensely that she gives little or no energy to encouraging her husband in his life work. A woman must never allow herself to become her husband's rival. His success is her primary concern.

6. So far, we have looked at God's ideal. But in Genesis 3, the first human tragedy altered things. How did Eve's disobedience affect her relationship to God (Genesis 3:1-13)?

_____

_____

1. Richard Francis Weymouth, *The New Testament in Modern Speech*, 3d ed., ed. and rev. Ernest Hampden-Cook (Boston: Pilgrim, n.d.).
2. From *Matthew Henry's Commentary on the Whole Bible.* Copyright © 1961 by Zondervan Publishing House and is used by permission.

To her husband? _____

_____

7. In what ways do women suffer today because of the failure of our first mother (Genesis 3:16; 1 *Timothy 2:11-15*)?

_____

_____

OBSERVATION: Though woman must now be subject to her husband, she still needs and wants what he has to offer— strength, protection, guidance, and authority.

8. Did God intend for a man's headship in marriage to become a dictatorship (1 Corinthians 7:3-4; Ephesians 5:22-23)?

_____

Note the equal responsibility of both partners and the final seat of authority.

9. How do you think God intends a woman to relate to men other than her husband in matters of leadership and authority?

_____

_____

10. Woman's job is no less important to God than man's. In Matthew 20:25-28, Jesus gave His disciples a prescription for greatness. What does this say to the woman who feels a position of servitude to man insults her worth as an individual?

_____

_____

What about differences in sex roles? How do they fit into God's plan? In our attempt to make all human beings free and equal, should we try to obliterate these role distinctions? Is there room for changes in roles, or are they meant to be fixed?

_____

_____

_____

11. Genesis 4:1-16 tells the awful story of grief that followed in the lives of Eve's children. How do you think Eve's disrupted relationship to her God affected her children?

_____

Do a woman's relationships to her husband and her God necessarily affect her relationships to her children? How are relationships interrelated?

_____

12. What reward awaits the woman who relates properly to God, husband, and children (Proverbs 31:28-31)? She shall be _____by her children (v. 28), _____ by her husband (v. 28), and _____ by her God (vv. 29-31).

OBSERVATION: Woman's reward is in direct proportion to her yieldedness to divine plan. She can be at her best only as she adheres to that tailor-made design.

GET THE POINT

Woman's place is under her God, beside her husband, and before her children, bringing glory to God in all her relationships.

Be Yourself

Lord, I want to be myself,
Different from my neighbor,
Doing what *I* want to do,
Giving vent to what *I* feel—
Unfettered,

16

Unhindered,
Untrapped,
Free!

Child, I want you to be yourself,
Different from your neighbor,
By following my master plan;
You're made to live that way—
Guided,
Helped,
Fulfilled,
Free!

FURTHER READING

Barclay, William. *The Letters to the Philippians, Colossians, and Thessalonians.* Philadelphia: Westminster, 1959. Pp. 192-94.
Henry, Matthew. *Matthew Henry's Commentary on the Whole Bible.* Grand Rapids: Zondervan, 1961. P. 7.
Hunt, Gladys. *Ms. Means My Self.* Grand Rapids: Zondervan, 1972.
Schaeffer, Edith. *Hidden Art.* Wheaton: Tyndale, 1971. Chapter 1.

2
Mary

INTRODUCING MARY

Mary of Nazareth picked her way through Jerusalem's timeworn streets. Under the afternoon sun, she wiped perspiration from her brow as she climbed the hill to the Temple.

From the Temple area up ahead, loud shouts and rumbling voices arrested her attention. People moved restlessly about one central point. Mary made out the forms of Temple officers on the fringe of the crowd. Unconsciously she tightened her shawl around her, as if to protect herself from these men who had brought so much grief to her tender, mother heart.

The rude officials broke into the crowd and shoved people back with sharp elbows. Moments later, Mary gasped to see them emerge with Peter and John between them.

Close on their heels appeared a beggar. His face was beaming, and he kept repeating, "Thanks be to God! An hour ago I couldn't walk. Now I can run and leap into the air!"

From remarks of the people around her as she approached, Mary pieced together the story. Peter and John had been going into the Temple to pray, when they came upon the beggar, lame from birth. He had called out for a coin, and Peter had said: "Silver and gold I do not have. But what I do have I give to you. In the name of Jesus of Nazareth, rise up and walk" (Acts 3:6, author's paraphrase).

Immediately the beggar had stood to his feet and walked, then leapt and run, rejoicing before the crowds in the Temple courts. When Peter had silenced the excited mob, he began to preach, insisting that Jesus was truly alive and had performed this remarkable act of healing. Such bold words had brought the angry Temple officers.

Mary caught a fleeting glimpse of Peter and John as their captors hustled them out of the courtyard. They were too far away to speak to her, but John's eyes met Mary's. They were triumphant. "Praise God!" they seemed to say. Something in John's manner checked the concern Mary felt in her heart.

As she entered the Temple, she recalled the first time she had walked there. It was the day she had brought her tiny son, Jesus, for His public presentation to the Lord

"To think," she said softly to herself, "that the greatest miracle of all time happened to me! For nine precious months I carried about in my body the Messiah of God. I was the channel for God's revelation of Himself to the world!"

Mary knelt and prayed, "Dear Father, thank You for giving me a part in Your greatest miracle. And for letting me see it reenacted in these last days. For every time You are invited into the life of a Peter or John, a beggar, a sinful woman, or—yes—even a Temple officer, it happens! You enter another human body, to live and move about—not just for nine months but for life. You give us all assurance and purpose for living! You reveal Your lovely nature to an unhappy, hate-filled world!"

WOMAN'S MISSION

Mary's life ushered in a new era in feminine history. While all womankind was represented by Eve, Mary introduced the amazing truth that women are important as individuals. It was many years before the value of woman's mission before God was recognized as being equal with that of man's mission. But with Mary, the seed of the idea was planted, and woman's new status began to grow.

1. God's plan has certain elements common to all people.

What are some of these (Matthew 28:19-20; Ephesians 2:10; 1 Timothy 2:4)?

_____

_____

Read Romans 12:3-8 and 1 Corinthians 12:4-6, 12-18. Do these verses indicate that God's plan is in all ways identical for all His children? What specific ministries and gifts does He give?

_____

_____

2. What was God's specific plan for Mary (Luke 1:26-33)?

_____

If God's timetable for earth and for the sending of His Son was established in eternity (see Galatians 4:4), do you think He had Mary chosen way back then, before the world was even created?

_____

EXTRA STUDY: Read the following Old Testament verses to learn some things God had predicted about the coming of His Son: Isaiah 7:14; 9:6; Micah 5:2.

3. Did Mary fully understand the angel's message (Luke 1:34)?

_____

Are we responsible to understand everything God asks of us before we obey Him (Proverbs 3:5-6)?

_____

OBSERVATION: When you send your child to bed at eight o'clock, you expect him to obey you on the basis of his confidence in your superior wisdom, not according to his immature understanding. God asks the same sort of obedience from us. He cannot always explain to us the reasons for His commands, but He asks us to trust His superior wisdom and act in confidence.

4. What does God give to those who trust when they cannot understand (Philippians 4:6-7)?

_____

5. What risks did Mary take in yielding her body to God to accomplish His plan through her (Matthew 1:18-19)?

_____

_____

How did God reward her faith and take care of Joseph's misgivings (Matthew 1:20-24)?

_____

_____

6. If yielding to God brings trouble, whose responsibility is it to work out the problems—ours or God's?

_____

OBSERVATION: Note how Mary felt about God once she had yielded to His plan (Luke 1:46-55). Resistance to God makes us bitter. Surrender leads to appreciation of His goodness, which we often express in worship.

7. How did God, through Mary, show Himself to the world (Luke 2:1-20; Philippians 2:5-11)?

_____

8. Did Mary trust and/or understand her son, according to Luke 2:41-52? _____

John 2:1-11? _____

John 19:25? _____

9. Mary was God's tool for accomplishing His purpose of the ages. After she had performed her task, how did Jesus show the value He placed on her as a person (John 19:25-27)?

_____

_____

OBSERVATION: Think how Mary's status improved after the crucifixion and resurrection of Jesus. As a member of the newly formed Church, she could enjoy constant fellowship with Him in prayer (Acts 1:13-14). Before, she wondered what God's plan for Him involved; now, with constantly renewed faith, she rejoiced at what that plan had accomplished for the world. Daily she carried on her God-given mission through prayer and a godly life.

10. How does God equip individual women today to do the variety of special jobs He includes in His mission for the Church (1 Corinthians 12:4-6; 12-18; 1 Peter 4:7-13)?

_____

_____

What part does suffering play in this process?

_____

Is trouble necessarily a tragedy (Psalm 46:1-11; 119:71-72; James 1:2-4)?

_____

OBSERVATION: An ancient Eastern proverb says, "All sunshine and no rain makes a desert."

11. If we meditate on the beauty of character the Lord wants to create in us through our obedience and sufferings, how will we react to life's pressures as we fulfill our mission (2 Corinthians 4:16-18)?

_____

GET THE POINT

Woman's mission in life is to yield herself to God—body, mind, emotions—so that through her He can show the world what He is like.

"I Do Love You"

"Mrs. Herr, you don't like me!"

Red-haired, freckle-faced Sammy Stevens wheeled and threw the words at me.

No child had ever told me that before. But neither had it been so true with any other child in my years of teaching experience. This boy's obnoxious behavior had annoyed me since the first day I had walked into that Sunday school classroom. Subconsciously I had hoped my feelings would not show; or, better yet, that he would stop coming. After all, how could I be expected to like Sammy Stevens?

But in my sudden consciousness of the truth, I felt a jab of conscience under the boy's angry stare. As a Sunday school teacher, my mission was to communicate the love of Christ to fifteen growing children—including Sammy Stevens!

And I had failed. *Come to think of it,* I realized, *I've never even prayed for anything so obvious as a change in my attitude.*

Then, as unexpectedly as the accusation had come, with its attendant wave of shame, a miracle occurred. Before I had a chance to verbalize my prayer, I sensed a power greater than my peevish self reaching down and lifting me up.

Putting my arm around the boy's tense shoulders, I looked into his defensive, hurt, blue eyes and said, "Yes, Sammy, I do like you. In fact I love you, and God loves you, too."

And in that speeding instant, I knew my heart was changed. For surging through me, I felt the love of God in a way I had never known before.

From that day on, Jesus Christ performed His mission through me in a new exciting way—even to Sammy Stevens!

FURTHER READING

Caswell, Helen Rayburn. *Jesus, My Son.* Richmond, Virginia: John Knox, 1962.

Deen, Edith. *The Bible's Legacy For Womanhood.* Garden City, N.Y.: Doubleday, 1969. Pp. 227, 232-35.

Holmes, Marjorie. *Two From Galilee.* Old Tappan, N.J.: Revell, 1972.

Lovelace, Delos W. *Journey to Bethlehem.* N.Y.: Crowell, 1953.

3
Jezebel

INTRODUCING JEZEBEL

Queen Jezebel stood erect in the doorway. For a moment she looked with amusement at her "royal" husband lying on his carved ivory bed, his face to the wall. Except for a few sniffles, he was silent.

She moved slowly toward him, holding her head with arrogant propriety. Standing directly over him, she spoke sharply. "What in all your kingdom so upsets you that you refuse food to come here and pout?"

As long as Jezebel had been married to Ahab, she had never gotten used to these sour, sullen spells of his. "Disgusting," she described them.

After a moment of dramatic silence, a muffled voice replied from the couch, "I asked Naboth to give me his vineyard, the one next to the palace grounds. I want it to plant an herb garden. I promised to pay him well, either with money or with another vineyard." *Sniffle.* "But he said no!"

The queen stared hard at Ahab. *What a spineless creature!* she thought. To her husband she shrieked, "Are you the ruler of this kingdom? You, who cower under the weak resistance of your poor subjects? How absurd even to bother asking Naboth about the matter, much less to offer him payment!"

She watched the little king with contempt as he stirred on his couch and half turned toward her. Perhaps he would defend himself? But no, instead he turned back to the wall once more and let silence reign. His resignation even to her tirades made Jezebel sick.

Addressing him as if he were a child, she wrapped the

matter up neatly: "Now, you coward, out of that bed with you! Eat and drink till your heart is merry. I shall get the vineyard for you."

Queen Jezebel gathered her trailing robes and swept confidently out the door. She hurried through the palace corridors, chuckling to herself in a cruel sort of way. *Weaklings! That's what these half-hearted followers of Jehovah are. How fortunate for me—and the cause of Baal worship!*

Now, my father was different, she remembered with a sense of admiration. *The great Eth-Baal, King of Tyre, who gained his throne through cold-blooded murder, was an iron-fisted ruler and devoted priest of Baal. He taught me well the passionate ways of Baal worship. His wisest move, though, was his alliance with Omri, King of Israel. As a seal of that otherwise insignificant treaty, I was given in marriage to Omri's son Ahab.*

Jezebel paused before the lavishly carved throne-room doors to recall her father's face. Smiling with satisfaction at his own importance, he had bid her farewell with these words: "Jezebel, my loyal daughter, I give to you the sacred task of destroying the worship of Jehovah God in Israel and of replacing it with your own religion of Baal and Astarte."

Then she entered the throne room, seated herself, and ordered a servant to write a death warrant for Naboth and his sons (on false charges, of course). Sealing the document with Ahab's signet ring, she delivered it to couriers with the instruction, "Speed the business to its conclusion!"

"And now, who is the real ruler of Israel?" she said aloud with pleasure. "With the temple of Baal erected at my request? With a host of idols and groves for practice of Baal's fertility and infant-sacrifice rites established throughout the kingdom? And even now as the order goes forth to arrest and execute Naboth, whose influence is greater—the God of Israel, or the gods of Jezebel?"

Her hollow laugh echoed and reechoed around the marble-paved hall.

WOMAN'S INFLUENCE

One of woman's greatest assets is her influence. She has a unique way of leaving the impress of her character and words upon every life she touches. She may inspire to great heights or drag to the lowest scum of earth's society. Strangely, she is often unaware of the operation of this powerful tool in her life.

While we can trace woman's influence through each of these studies, Jezebel stands out as perhaps the most obviously influential. As a contrast to her evil influence, we will look also at the virtuous woman described in Proverbs 31. Studying these two characters side by side will help us see how identical feminine resources can be used as tools for either good or evil.

1. What kind of a king was Ahab, Jezebel's husband? And what part did Jezebel play in his character development (1 Kings 21:25-26)?

_____

_____

2. Read Judges 16 and 1 Kings 11:1-11 for examples of other women with pagan philosophies who caused the downfall of strong, promising leaders. How would you say a woman's spiritual viewpoint affects the nature of her influence in other areas of life?

_____

_____

3. What influence did Jezebel's Baal worship have on the character of her daily life (1 Kings 18:19)?

_____

_____

Read Proverbs 31:10-31. How would you say the virtuous woman's influence differs from Jezebel's?

_____

_____

OBSERVATION: The influence of our daily lives is one of the things to which we give the least thought. Yet it is the area of greatest impact upon others, the area that never stops working.

4. A wife's mission is to encourage her husband, without preaching or nagging, in the ways of divine wisdom. Read 1 Kings 21:1-24 and note how Jezebel's words, backed with actions, brought ruin to Ahab. How can a woman's words destroy her husband (cf. James 3:2-12)?

How can they benefit him (Proverbs 31:11-12, 26)?

5. How does an ill-tempered, bossy woman influence others (Proverbs 21:9, 19; 27:15-16)?

6. Jezebel's distinction lies in her reputation for cruelty and lustful idolatry. By contrast, what sort of prestige does the virtuous woman enjoy (Proverbs 31:10-12, 28-31)?

7. Upon what did Jezebel rely to gain her desired ends (2 Kings 9:30-31)?

What was the result of her actions (vv. 32-37)?

How can physical charm be dangerous (Proverbs 6:24-29)?

NOTE: Proverbs 6:20-23 is good advice for mothers to pass on to their sons about defending themselves against the influences of vain, physical beauty.
8. How does the virtuous woman regard both physical appearances and inner, spiritual beauty (Proverbs 31:22, 25)?

NOTE: The story of Jezebel's children tells us much about the influence of her motherhood (see 1 Kings 22:51-53; 2 Kings 3:1-3; 8:16-18).

After the reign of King Solomon, the nation of Israel had been divided into two kingdoms: Israel in the north and Judah in the south. Often hostility developed between the two kingdoms.

On one occasion, King Ahab made an alliance with the God-fearing King Jehoshaphat of Judah. Ahab and Jezebel sealed this alliance by giving in marriage their daughter Athaliah to Judah's crown prince, Jehoram. Through the influence of this ungodly daughter of Jezebel, the worship of Baal was tolerated in Judah. Thus, Jezebel had sowed the seed that led to Judah's moral decline and national destruction three hundred years later. (See 2 Chronicles 21-23 for a detailed account.)

9. Can a godly woman have as strong an influence on her children as a mother like Jezebel (Proverbs 22:6)?

_____

10. In the tribute to Jezebel (2 Kings 9:34), what one word best describes her influence on others?

_____

What contrasting word in Proverbs 31:28 describes the virtuous woman?

_____

11. Is it possible for a woman to live her life without influencing others (Romans 14:7; 1 Corinthians 12:20-26)?

_____

How can she use that influence to effect the greatest good in the world (Romans 6:12-13; 12:1)?

_____

GET THE POINT

The godly woman's influence flows from her Christ-controlled personality. Recognizing her influence as a gift from God, she yields it to Him for His perfect use.

Instrument

Influence is yours,
Working woman, mother, wife.
Use it to impress—
Pattern of God's holiness,
Instrument of heaven's love.

FURTHER READING

Deen, Edith. *Family Living In the Bible*. N.Y.: Harper & Row, 1963. Pp. 62, 68-70, 182-3.

Douglas, J. D., ed. *The New Bible Dictionary*. Grand Rapids: Eerdmans, 1962. Pp. 20, 634.

Hall, Newton Marshall and Wood, Irving Francis. *The Book of Life*, Vol. 3, *Bible Kings, Captains*. 25th ed. Chicago: John Rudin, 1948. Pp. 346-7.

Halley, Henry H. *Bible Handbook*. Chicago: Halley, 1959. Pp. 187, 189, 210.

Henry, Matthew. *Matthew Henry's Commentary on the Whole Bible*. Grand Rapids: Zondervan, 1961. Pp. 387-97, 413.

The New Scofield Reference Bible. N.Y.: Oxford U., 1967. P. 434.

Price, Eugenia. *Beloved World*. Grand Rapids: Zondervan, 1961. Chapter 18.

_____. *Woman to Woman*. Grand Rapids: Zondervan, 1959. Chapter 1.

4
Rahab

INTRODUCING RAHAB

Rahab the harlot was not normally frightened by men. Her name, meaning "proud," was well known to the men of Jericho. A cheerful young woman, she was a natural for her job. She had every reason to be proud of the rare, feminine beauty and subtle charms with which she relaxed her patrons' tensions.

But today Rahab greeted the two strangers at her door with genuine fear. They were not here on her kind of business. Theirs was a secret mission. They were wild men from the desert, part of a massive invasion of several millions of people (Israelites by name), moving in from Egypt.

Everywhere they went, these people left behind them a story of uncanny conquest. In the name of their invisible God, Jehovah, they accomplished superhuman feats of war—though there was not a trained soldier among them!

For some time it had been rumored that Jehovah had promised to give them all the cities and villages of Canaan. For several weeks, the people of Jericho had whispered the news to one another, until the city was in a state of hysteria. As Israel marched closer, suspicion grew that Jericho would be the first target of attack. Then, as if to confirm the horrifying suspicions, the vast horde camped just opposite Jericho, across the Jordan River.

Like her neighbors, Rahab lived in a state of tension. Even their temple priests gave them no hope. Almost certainly the God of Israel had a magical power superior to the gods of Jericho. The people of Jericho knew the situation was hopeless. No matter how strong its walls, the city and all who lived in it lay under a death sentence!

Trembling now, Rahab looked at the two men on her doorstep. Spies, looking for refuge! And what would be her fate if she were convicted of hiding them? Certain death!

Which would be worse? she wondered. To die at the hand of her leaders now, or at their side on the day of battle? In either case, her doom was sealed. Unless—

Her eyes brightened with hope. What if she made a bargain with Jehovah's spies—her life for their refuge?

She felt her fear slowly loosen its paralyzing grip. Rahab the harlot opened wide her door and welcomed in two strange and frightening men. Messengers of death they were. Or could they be, at least for her, deliverers?

WOMAN'S HOPE

> Hope is
> groping my way
> through a tunnel so dark
> I've no idea who or what
> goes with me there;
> Then spotting,
> in the far-off distance,
> a tiny prick of light,
> sparkling like a diamond:
> Promise of relief!

The presence of hope implies that we are dissatisfied with our lot and anticipate an improvement.

In studying Rahab, we will examine the hopelessness of her situation. Then we will watch how God fanned the tiny flame of hope flickering in her heart into a brightly burning torch which she passed on to others.

1. First, think about the word *hope*. What does it mean to you?

_____

_____

Where does hope come from (See Psalm 39:7; cf. *Jeremiah* 17:7-8)?

_____

_____

NOTE: In biblical usage of the word, hope nearly always connotes pleasure and confidence as well as anticipation.

2. What does Joshua 2:1-7 tell us about Rahab's occupation and character?

_____

How would you expect these things to help or hinder her hopes for deliverance during the planned destruction of Jericho?

_____

_____

NOTE: The position of a harlot was quite respectable in Jericho, as well as in most heathen societies of that day. Often the priestesses of Canaanite deities served as public prostitutes, to help support the temples. Rahab may have served in this capacity. Many modern scholars, however, question whether the word used for "harlot" here had the same connotation as it does for us today.

3. What had the people of Jericho heard about Israel, and how did they react to the news (Joshua 2:8-11)?

_____

_____

EXTRA STUDY: You can read in Exodus 14 and Numbers 21:21-35 about the events Rahab cited.

NOTE: The heathen nations identified each other with their patron gods. Hence, they attributed Israel's victories to Jehovah, her God. They recognized that a God who could accomplish the things mentioned in Joshua 2:10 must be more powerful than their own gods.

4. According to Psalm 56:3-4, fear can be helpful if it leads us to do what?

_____

What then happens to our fear?

_____

5. On what did Rahab base her hope for deliverance (Joshua 2:11b-13)?

_____

What conditions did the men give her for being rescued (Joshua 2:14-21)?

_____

_____

OBSERVATION: Many Bible teachers see in this scarlet cord a picture of the blood of Jesus Christ that saves us from our sins. Compare Exodus 12:1-13 with John 1:29 and 1 Peter 1:18-19.

6. For what real reason did God spare Rahab and her family? Was it her act of obedience (Joshua 6:17, 23-25) or was there something deeper that prompted that obedience (Hebrews 11:31; James 2:24-26)?

_____

7. To what new life and special honor did Rahab's faith lead her (Joshua 6:25; Matthew 1:1-6)? Note that the name sometimes translated *Rachab* is the same as *Rahab*.

_____

NOTE: Whenever a woman's name is included in a genealogical listing in Jewish history, you can be sure she has made a significant contribution to her generation. To be a part of the genealogical listing of Jesus, the Son of God, was indeed a high honor. Only four women are included in this list, each having played a unique role in preparing the world for God's Son.

8. Rahab became the mother of Boaz, who married Ruth. We will meet this man in the next lesson. But it is important to note here that though Boaz lived at a time when moral standards had dropped very low in Israel, yet he was an unusual example of high, moral principles. What does this suggest to you of character change in Rahab?

_____

9. In God's sight, is anyone good enough to have no need to hope for His forgiveness (Romans 3:10-12, 23)?

Is anyone too bad to claim God's forgiveness (Isaiah 55:6-9; Romans 10:13)?

10. Consider these statements: (1) There is no rank at the foot of the cross. (2) We can have hope in God only when we recognize our hopelessness without Him. What do these statements imply about the attitude we should maintain toward apparently hopeless sinners (see also Matthew 9:10-13; Galatians 6:1-2)?

11. How can a woman today receive hope for a new life from God (Matthew 11:28-30; John 1:12; 2 Corinthians 5:17)?

GET THE POINT

Woman's hope is to find Christ forgiving and satisfying at every point of failure and hopelessness in life.

Hope

Hope is
　Sitting by the bedside
　　Of my child;
　Touching his little hand
　　So limp and pale,
　Like the first advance
　　Of creeping death;
　Watching for a sign of life
　　To break the long,
　　　Unconscious spell;
　And seeing it—
　　An eyelid flutters,
　　Opens a wee crack,
　And shows my boy's still there.

Hope is
    Being hurt by dear ones,
    Smarting at the blows
        That wound, then crush my human spirit,
    Until I can no longer trust
        A single living soul,
        And I despair.
    Then God steps in
        And sends me one of His own children,
        To smile
        And listen,
        Bear my burdens with me,
        Prove he's worthy of my trust.

Hope is
    Bearing a daily load
        Of guilt,
    Trying to black out from my memory
        The things I've done—
            Big, ugly faults,
            Petty, little aggravations
                That lead to family tizzies—
        Yet going on, repeating them,
        Adding new sins to the list;
    Then stopping for a moment
        To read these special words:
            "Come unto me,
            I'll give you rest,"
    And lifting up my heart
        To say:
            "God, take it all—
                My sin,
                My hurried, worried self.
        I can't; You can.
        Oh, thank You, Lord."

FURTHER READING

Douglas, J. D., ed. *The New Bible Dictionary*. Grand Rapids: Eerdmans, 1962. Pp. 611-13, 1048.
Halley, Henry H. *Bible Handbook*. Chicago: Halley, 1959. P. 152.

Marshall, Catherine. *Beyond Ourselves*. New York: McGraw-Hill, 1961. Chapter 10.

Price, Eugenia. *Beloved World*. Grand Rapids: Zondervan, 1961. Chapter 12.

5
Ruth

INTRODUCING RUTH

The midnight silence of Naomi's little house was so oppressive that even the beating of Ruth's heart seemed smothered. From somewhere out in the night, she heard a dog bark. Then all was still again.

Head propped up on her hands, Ruth the Moabitess watched a silvery path of moonlight stream through the narrow window and across the foot of her bed. She kicked restlessly at her homespun coverlet. The harder she tried to dismiss the memories that darted through her mind, the more vivid they became.

She was a child again, bowing to the statue of the god Chemosh; wondering when he would ask her parents to offer her to his sacrificial furnace; listening to the terrifying wails and shouts of drunken neighbors dancing far into the night in the groves of the village images! She felt again the choking fear of everything religious.

Then she saw him—Mahlon, the Hebrew. Strange fellow he was, thin and pale. But there was something mysteriously attractive about him, something she had not begun to understand until she met his mother. For Naomi was the kindest, purest woman she had ever known—the sort of woman she herself longed to be.

She smiled at the memory of her unlikely marriage. Ruth had felt genuinely proud to be accepted into this special family, for no Hebrew would normally think of marrying a Moabitess!

Now Mahlon was dead! He, his brother, and their father—all three had been stricken by the judgment of their strange God. Or so Naomi had insisted: "It was because we left Judah to come live in Moab."

Ruth began to sob. By custom she was expected to live with Naomi, until she had found another husband. But tomorrow Naomi was returning to Bethlehem. How could she follow her there? She would have to adopt the ways and ideas of the Hebrews. Still they would despise her and probably never allow her to marry. All because she was a Moabitess!

"Oh, why?" she wondered aloud.

The moon had risen until it was now shining fully in Ruth's face. "A perfect creation of Jehovah, God of Israel," Mahlon would say if he were here.

Is it possible, the young woman asked herself, *that this firm insistence on the worship of the invisible God Jehovah is after all the thing that makes Mahlon's family and his nation what they are?*

Suddenly it seemed to her that the issue she faced was simple. She must choose not between families or nations. The question was, Which god would she serve, Chemosh or Jehovah?

At the thought of Chemosh, Ruth knew her answer. She had never really wanted to belong to that heathen deity. She had always rebelled. And tonight, more than anything else, she wanted to belong to the God of Israel, the God of Mahlon and Naomi.

Ruth turned her slender body over and lay face down on her sleeping mat. Clasping clammy hands high above her head, she cried, "Oh, God of Israel. I know your ways of judgment against your enemies such as my people, Moab. Now, let me suffer shame and loneliness the rest of my days. Yes, kill me if you like! But never ask me to return to Chemosh! I will follow Naomi to Bethlehem and I will follow you to death!"

Exhausted from the struggle, at peace in her decision, Ruth closed her eyes and was soon breathing with the gentle rhythm of sleep.

Faith, like hope, begins with need. If a woman has no need, why trust anyone outside herself? So, as we did with Rahab, we will look first at Ruth's difficult situation. Then we can trace the growth of her faith.

To better understand this lesson, read through the entire book of Ruth for an overview of the story. It is short and will take only a few minutes.

1. What restriction had God placed upon His people's association with the people of Moab? For what reasons (Deuteronomy 23:3-6)?

_____

NOTE: While the Israelites were traveling in the desert, Balak, King of Moab, had become frightened of them (as did the Jerichoites, later). Being a superstitious man, he had hired a powerful prophet named Balaam to go out and pronounce a curse on Israel. Because of this act and the extreme wickedness of the Moabitish people, God insisted on Israel's strict separation from them. You can read the full story of Balaam in Numbers 22-24.

2. Read Ruth 1:1-13, noting why Naomi's family moved to Moab and what happened to them there. As Naomi prepared to return to Bethlehem, do you think she was wise or unwise to discourage the two young widows from returning with her?

_____

OBSERVATION: Consider three conflicting factors Naomi must have found difficulty in reconciling: (1) her cultural obligation to care for her widowed daughters-in-law until they found husbands; (2) her destitute state in Moab, with neither husband nor sons to support her; and (3) the certainty that Ruth and Orpah would not be accepted in Bethlehem.

3. What do Orpah's choice and the hesitancy with which

she made it tell us about her faith and loyalty (Ruth 1:10, 14-15)?

_____

_____

4. When Ruth declared her intention of accompanying Naomi, what changes in her life and faith was she prepared to make (Ruth 1:15-18)?

_____

_____

5. According to Romans 10:11-13, is there any restriction as to the kinds of people God will accept?

_____

What are His conditions for acceptance?

_____

6. What provisions had God made for the livelihood of the poor (Deuteronomy 24:19-22)?

_____

7. How did Ruth prove the reality of her new faith (Ruth 2:1-13)?

_____

What was her reward (Ruth 2:14-23)?

_____

OBSERVATION: Ruth discovered the beautiful truth that all God's laws are subject to His highest laws of justice and love.
8. Read Deuteronomy 25:5-10 for the description of the Hebrew custom Naomi referred to in Ruth 3:1-4. It provided for the redemption (or restoration) of a dead man's family lineage. What specific instructions did Naomi give Ruth in Ruth 3:1-4?

_____

_____

NOTE: Naomi's suggestion is shocking to us. But this was a properly conducted custom of the day. Ruth, as a widow, was expected to take the initiative in asking her deceased husband's next-of-kin to marry her. The practice of the man spreading his garment over the woman (Ruth 3:6-9) was a token of his intention to protect her. It was comparable to the giving of an engagement ring in our society.

9. What was the full reward of Ruth's faith (Ruth 4:13-17; Matthew 1:1, 5. See note in Lesson 4, question 7)?

_____

_____

Both Rahab and Ruth reached out to God in hope and faith and were identified with Jesus in His ancestral line, even though they came from Gentile, heathen nations!

10. According to Romans 3:23 and Ezekiel 18:4b, the curse of spiritual death rests on all of mankind. Who alone is able to deliver us from the curse of sin and restore us to right relations with God, as pictured in Boaz's redemption of Ruth (Acts 4:12; Galatians 3:13)?

_____

11. What is faith (Hebrews 11:1)?

_____

How can it be obtained (Romans 10:17)?

_____

What part does it play in changing our relationship to God (Hebrews 11:6)?

_____

12. For an interesting and enlightening study, read Hebrews 11, often called the "faith chapter." Note the variety of people listed in this heavenly "hall of fame." Think of people you have known personally whose names you think

would be included if God were to revise this list tomorrow. Would He add your name?

Woman's faith is the vehicle to bring her to God, when she trusts in His goodness rather than her own worthiness.

Faith Is A Little Child

The idea of climbing those nineteen stairs for the second time in a half hour was irksome, indeed. But it had to be done. From the bedroom overhead I heard childish giggles and squeaky bedsprings instead of the peaceful silence which would have indicated naps progressing as ordered.

So, moments later, still a little out of breath from the climb, I sat on the edge of four-year-old Martha's bed and began my lecture on the evils of nap evasion. I was promptly interrupted, however, by two-year-old Tim's voice from the next bed.

"Mommie, my heart is dirty."

I stopped in midsentence and turned to stare at him. Could he know what he was talking about? Was it possible he had caught the meaning of the black page in the Wordless Book I had been teaching to Martha? Did he really connect it with his sin of disobedience at naptime?

I hesitated a minute, inclined to ignore what I felt sure must have been meaningless chatter. But Tim persisted, repeating his confession. So, fearful of ruining an opportunity for learning, I asked, "What are you going to do about it?"

"Give it to Jesus," was the sober reply.

I gulped. "And what will He do with it?"

"Clean it up, like the book says."

He must mean the red page, representing the blood of Christ, I decided.

Still unbelieving, I helped him with a simple prayer.

"Dear Jesus, my heart is dirty. I'm sorry. Please clean it up. Amen."

He repeated it after me, one phrase at a time, concluding

with, "Amen. It's clean now, Mommie, like the white page." His upturned face was shining. "And Jesus is building me a house in heaven right now."

"Like the gold page?" I asked.

"Um-hm." His blond head nodded. Then he turned over and fell asleep.

It was months before I let myself believe that tiny toddler had meant business with God. But Tim never forgot, and at last I had to admit his conversion was for real.

And that is the way I learned that faith is a little child—or his childlike mother—saying, "Dear God, my heart is dirty. Please clean it up."

FURTHER READING

McGee, J. Vernon. *Ruth: The Romance of Redemption*. Findlay, Ohio: Dunham, 1962.

Price, Eugenia. *Beloved World*. Grand Rapids: Zondervan, 1961. Chapter 14.

_____. *God Speaks To Women Today*. Grand Rapids: Zondervan, 1964. Chapter 9.

_____. *Woman to Woman*. Grand Rapids: Zondervan, 1959. Chapter 14.

Reeve, Pamela. *Faith Is...* Portland, Ore.: Multnomah, 1970.

Ruth, A Bible Suede-Graph for the Flannelboard. Wheaton, Ill.: Scripture Press, 1959. Pp. 3-4.

6
Mary Magdalene

INTRODUCING MARY MAGDALENE

Mary of Magdala sat near the window. She gazed admiringly at Jesus, and spoke more to herself than to the woman next to her. "How much He loves them all!"

It was a hot summer day in Galilee. Jesus had been invited into this humble home to teach about the Kingdom of God. But His visit was no secret to the neighbors. Shortly, the whole town arrived to swarm through the doors.

Mary watched the poor folk in tattered rags push close to Him. She caught glimpses of children peeking between robes to look on the Master's face. Glancing out the window, she spotted a few elite citizens skirting the edge of the crowd that overflowed far into the street.

In her heart she felt a twinge of pain at the sight of religious men in immaculate robes. Scorn was written across their pious faces as they gazed at the helpless wretches shoving their impatient way toward the little house.

Turning again from the window, Mary felt the closeness of the stifling air heavy with the odors of sweating bodies, open sores, roaming dogs. She watched Peter, John, and Andrew holding back the crowds lest they trample Jesus to death.

Suddenly a sharp scream broke her reverie as it cut through low, rumbling noises of the throng. The words were distorted, almost unintelligible: "This man is Jesus, Son of the most high God!"

From the back of the room, came a raving maniac, arms thrashing wildly. People all around backed into each other to make way for her.

Mary gasped and shut her eyes. Clasping her hands in her lap, she sat motionless. In the months she had been traveling with Jesus' party, she had never become used to these dreadful encounters with Satan. She knew what Jesus would do. He would rebuke the evil spirit in the woman. It would throw her to the floor and leave her limp and senseless.

Then, remembering the warmth of that first touch of Jesus' hand on her own ruined body, she opened her eyes. Yes, He was touching this young woman out of whom He had just cast a demon. Mary felt a tingle of relieved delight. Instinctively, she stepped forward and reached out to steady the woman now rising to her feet.

Mary's eyes were misty as she heard those same lips that had moments earlier raved so madly, now speaking coherently: "Thank You, Master. Oh, thank You!"

Mary drew the woman toward her. Pushing back the tousled hair from the tired face, she led her out of the house, away from the crowds. At a distant, quiet spot, she could share her own special story, explain her own deep gratitude.

WOMAN'S GRATITUDE

Gratitude is an attitude:
A heart so richly blessed
It fairly bursts,
Anxious to say,
In simple word
Or kindly deed,
"Thank you, my friend;
Your life has filled mine
To the brim."

When a woman puts her faith in Jesus Christ, He rewards that trust. But this is only the beginning. If her faith is centered in Him as a Person, a new relationship develops. She begins giving Him her faithful devotion, motivated by gratitude for all He has done for her.

1. What special thing had Christ done for Mary (Luke 8:1-2)?

NOTE: When Jesus lived on earth, Satan was especially active in possessing people. This demon possession took many forms. Sometimes it caused physical illness; often, severe psychological and moral disorders resulted. We do not know in what form Mary's possession manifested itself. OBSERVATION: Luke 8:2 says she had had seven devils. The number seven, in the Bible, stands for completeness. The implication may be that Mary was completely possessed—and completely delivered!

2. While most people are not possessed by Satan as was Mary Magdalene, all are naturally subject, at least in part, to Satan and his sinful designs (see John 8:34; Romans 6:16). How can we be delivered from Satan's power to force us to sin (Romans 6:5-14)?

---

3. For an in-depth consideration of this subject, study Romans 6-8. Note Paul's grateful reaction when he realized he had been delivered from Satan's dominion (Romans 7:24-25a).

4. In what practical way did Mary Magdalene express her gratitude to Jesus (Luke 8:1-3)?

NOTE: Many Bible scholars believe Mary had been a wealthy woman of high social position before her demon possession. After her healing, she and the other women mentioned in Luke 8 accompanied Jesus and His disciples on their preaching tours. They probably prepared the men's meals and did their laundry, even paying for the group's needs from their own pockets.

OBSERVATION: Jesus came into this world to serve, not to be served (see Mark 10:45). But the grateful women in His life did minister to His material needs, thus freeing Him to accomplish His great spiritual purposes.

5. Where was Mary in Jesus' darkest hour, when all His disciples had forsaken Him (John 19:25)?

_____

OBSERVATION: Without Jesus, Mary's life was meaningless. She did not fear the Jewish leaders. All she desired was to fulfill the impulses of her gratitude and to minister to Jesus' needs up to the end.

6. How did Mary serve Jesus at His burial (Mark 15:40—16:1)? _____

7. When the others had all gone back to the city after finding Jesus' tomb empty, where did Mary linger (John 20:10-11)? _____ Why do you think she did this?

_____

Read carefully John 20:14-18, and try to project yourself into this special moment between Mary and Jesus.

8. What unique distinction did Mary enjoy (Mark 16:9)?

_____

NOTE: Some versions omit Mark 16:9-20. Verse 9 reads: "But He arose to life early on the first day of the week, and appeared first to Mary of Magdala from whom He had expelled seven demons" (Weymouth[1]).

Why was this privilege reserved for Mary?

_____

9. The Bible is filled with admonitions to give thanks to the Lord. According to Hebrews 13:15, how often should we do this?

_____

10. Read Psalm 103. List the things David mentions for which we should give thanks. Then make a list of blessings from your own personal life.

_____   _____

1. Richard Francis Weymouth, *The New Testament in Modern Speech*, 3d ed., ed. and rev. Ernest Hampden-Cook (Boston: Pilgrim, n.d.).

_____ _____
_____ _____
_____ _____
_____ _____

11. Does God expect us to rejoice and give thanks even in times of suffering, difficulty, and bereavement (*Matthew 5:10-12*; 1 Thessalonians 5:16-18; James 1:2-4)?

_____

OBSERVATION: The men in the Bible who praised God the most were men who suffered the most. David wrote many of his comforting psalms in cold, dark caves of refuge, while running for his life. Paul, who suffered much persecution, either thanked God for some blessing or commanded the churches to do so forty-four times in the thirteen letters he wrote. Job praised God while lying in an ash heap and scraping his boils.

12. Mere words are not an adequate expression of real gratitude to God. Jot a list of practical ways you can show your gratitude in daily life. (See Psalm 50:14; Matthew 25:31-46; Romans 12:1.)

_____

_____

GET THE POINT

Woman's gratitude is centered in what Jesus has done for her. It expresses itself in complete identification with and service to Him.

Gratitude

O God, Thou art my God; I shall seek Thee earnestly;
My soul thirsts for Thee, my flesh yearns for Thee,
In a dry and weary land where there is no water.
Thus I have beheld Thee in the sanctuary,
To see Thy power and Thy glory.

Because Thy lovingkindness is better than life,
My lips shall praise Thee.
So I will bless Thee as long as I live;
I will lift up my hands in Thy name.
My soul is satisfied as with marrow and fatness,
And my mouth offers praises with joyful lips.

When I remember Thee on my bed,
I meditate on Thee in the night watches,
For Thou hast been my help,
And in the shadow of Thy wings I sing for joy.
My soul clings to Thee;
Thy right hand upholds me.[2]

Psalm 63:1-8, NASB

FURTHER READING

Butler, J. Glentworth. *Butler's Bible Work: The Gospels.*
New York: Funk & Wagnall, 1889. Sections 46, 161.
Douglas, J. D., ed. *The New Bible Dictionary.* Grand Rapids:
Eerdman's, 1962. Pp. 792-93.
Farrar, F. W. *The Life of Christ.* London: Cassell, n.d. Chapters 21-22.
Marshall, Peter. *The First Easter.* New York: McGraw-Hill,
1959.
Price, Eugenia. *Beloved World.* Grand Rapids: Zondervan,
1961. Chapter 56.
_____. *God Speaks To Women Today.* Grand Rapids: Zondervan, 1964. Chapter 21.

2. New American Standard Bible, © The Lockman Foundation, 1960, 1962, 1963, 1968, 1971, 1972, 1973. Used by permission.

7
Daughters of Zion

INTRODUCING THE DAUGHTERS OF ZION

Bright lines of pink and gold streaked through the hot western sky. Soft breezes swayed the palm fronds overhead and played with the folds of Mrs. Isaiah's blue shawl.

The woman held herself erect and walked with confident stride through sandy streets. Other women were coming, too, to draw their daily supply of water from the Judean village well. Laughing and talking together, noisily they tripped along. Dainty gold bands jangled about their ankles. Strong scents of perfume were wafted on gentle puffs of wind. Little dust clouds swirled around the hems of their fine-spun garments.

"What a fashion parade, this daily visit to the well!" Mrs. Isaiah commented to an older woman walking by her side.

"Yes," replied her companion. "Their heads are full of their own importance. But their hearts are empty; for they only pretend to worship God."

"My husband says God will judge Judah, in part because of the waywardness of the women." Mrs. Isaiah's beautiful eyes were sober as she spoke.

The two women stood by the well now, easing heavy, clay water jugs off their shoulders.

"Your husband's words are not idle, my dear," said the older woman. "Remember, he has received them from God."

As Mrs. Isaiah dropped her jug over the edge of the well and let out the cord, one of the younger women sidled up to her. Throwing back her head and gesturing toward Mrs.

Isaiah, she shouted dramatically: "Behold the prophetess of doom! Too pious even to wear a little good-luck charm around her neck to protect her from her husband's predicted judgment."

Laughter burst from the crowd. Mocking words hurled through the air.

"She lives by her grandmother's codes!"

"She would make us the laughingstock of our neighboring countries!"

"Only a bore like Isaiah would marry such a prude!"

The prophetess shouldered her load of water and then paused. The women fell silent as she spoke:

"How I wish your hearts were half as lovely as the ornaments on your bodies. You have forgotten Solomon's wise words: 'Charms are deceptive and beauty is short lived; but a woman that commits herself to the Lord, she shall know enduring glory' " (Proverbs 31:30, author).

Again a shower of taunting insults. The two women walked calmly through the hilarious crowd.

"How can it be?" Mrs. Isaiah mused. "Isaiah says *all* our sons were named by God to speak of Judah's future. *Maher-shalal-hash-baz* (judgment comes speedily), I can believe. Other prophets, too, have spoken this message. But *Shear-jashub* (a remnant shall return) seems so remote."

The older woman smiled. "But God has promised a special child, to be named 'Immanuel.' "

"Oh yes! *Immanuel* (God with us)! If this is true, if God is truly with us, perhaps there is hope. For He can lift us up even when we have fallen."

WOMAN'S DOWNFALL

While God has a perfect plan for each woman He creates, He never forces that plan on any of us. In Isaiah's day most of the women of the nation of Judah had forsaken God and His plan. They were following their own self-made patterns of life. In this lesson, we will trace their downfall back to its original causes and see if we can discover how to avoid their mistakes.

1. For what special purpose had God chosen Israel as a nation (later divided into Israel and Judah) (Exodus 19:5-6;

Deuteronomy 7:6)? Note that the word *peculiar* used in some versions does not mean "odd" but "distinctive" or "unique."

OBSERVATION: God chose the people of Israel to be His special representatives on earth. Their primary mission was to spread the knowledge of Jehovah, the one true God, to the rest of the world. Note that when God called Abraham to be the father of this nation (Genesis 12:1-3), He spoke of them as being an avenue of blessing to the whole world.
What happened to the relationship between God and His people (Isaiah 1:2-4)?

OBSERVATION: Throughout the Old Testament, God compares His relationship to Israel with a marriage. Unfaithfulness to God is described as spiritual adultery. God's people never set out deliberately to reject Him. Rather, they let neighboring nations gradually influence them to worship idols and then to lower their moral standards.
Read Ezekiel 16:1-43 for a pathetically vivid picture of Israel's unfaithfulness. Here God speaks as the rejected husband of His beloved bride.
2. Why did Judah's worship displease God (Isaiah 1:11-17; 2:5-11; *cf. 1 Samuel 15:22*)?

NOTE: Even though Judah had rejected God as a Person, they went on observing many of His prescribed forms of worship. They hoped this would satisfy His demands and induce Him to be lenient with their unfaithfulness of heart.
3. How do we sometimes make our worship unacceptable to God? _____
4. What judgments did God warn would be brought against the "daughters of Zion" (Isaiah 3:16—4:1)?

OBSERVATION: God will not judge a whole nation for the sins of her women alone. But women, with their strong influence, can easily determine a nation's moral direction and thus bring about either national blessing or national downfall.

5. In what ways is modern society (community, home, and church) being influenced morally and spiritually by today's women?

_____

_____

6. Read 1 Samuel 16:7. In the light of this truth about how God looks at us, would you say the real sin of these women in Isaiah's time was the wearing of the ornaments listed in Isaiah 3, or something deeper?

_____

What was their deep sin (Isaiah 3:16)? _____

_____

7. How does God feel about the sin of arrogant pride (Proverbs 6:16-17; 1 Peter 5:5-6)?

_____

To what does it inevitably lead (Proverbs 16:18)?

_____

OBSERVATION: Selfish pride is at the root of nearly all sin. Gradually such a haughty spirit leads us to turn our backs on God entirely, as we rob Him of His glory and give it to ourselves.

8. How can we be alert to symptoms of pride in our lives? _____

What practical steps can we take to keep selfish pride from determining our behavior patterns (Philippians 2:3-8)?

_____

_____

9. What remedy did God offer for Judah's moral sickness (Isaiah 1:16-19; 2:5)?

_____

_____

OBSERVATION: Because God is holy and just, He must pronounce and execute judgment. But because He is love, He always tempers His pronouncements with pleas for repentance and offers of forgiveness.

According to Isaiah 4:4-6, God promised that when the judgment was over, the work of His hands would be their new "pride and adornment." What a fantastic exchange! True spiritual beauty for exterior charms! "Beauty for ashes" (Isaiah 61:3).

10. How is our relationship to God similar to that of Israel (or Judah), once we have trusted Christ as Saviour (Titus 2:11-14)?

_____

_____

What things in God's message to Judah can we apply to ourselves (see 1 Corinthians 10:1-13)?

_____

_____

Note how God appeals to us, His spiritual people, when we fail to live up to His desires for us (Revelation 3:15-21).

11. What is one of the best ways to keep our hearts from being gradually drawn away into unfaithfulness (1 John 1:9)?

_____

OBSERVATION: The Christian life is like the sketching of a landscape. If we correct each error as it is penciled in, the picture will never become so confused that it has to be done over from scratch.

54

GET THE POINT

Woman's downfall is the exaltation of herself rather than her God; fashioning her life by the standards of her peers rather than by God's Word; refusing to confess these failings as sins and forsake them.

Confession

Lord, tonight I'm disappointed
in people,
    circumstances,
    feelings,
and *myself*.

I'm feeling blue,
    frustrated,
    sad, and irritated
by people,
    circumstances,
    feelings,
and *myself*.

Lord, as You look on me
and watch my bungling
    touchiness
    and anger,
are You disappointed, too—
    disappointed as I,
    in *myself*?

FURTHER READING

Douglas, J. D., ed. *The New Bible Dictionary*. Grand Rapids: Eerdman's, 1962. Pp. 34, 631.
Price, Eugenia. *Woman to Woman*. Grand Rapids: Zondervan, 1959. Chapter 7.

8
Hannah

INTRODUCING HANNAH

Eli, the aging high priest, sat beside a post of the Temple in Shiloh. Rubbing his weary eyes, he thought to himself: *What a lot of people have come from every part of our little nation to worship Jehovah God on this feast day!*

It was Passover time. As usual the Temple priests were busier than at any other season. All day long they offered the people's sacrificial victims, as God had prescribed, for the forgiveness of sins.

The gray-bearded priest was startled when a veiled woman rushed into the Temple court. Throwing herself on the floor, she began to sob. Then, lifting her eyes upward, she seemed to be speaking. But though he strained his ears, Eli could not make out a word. Only an occasional choking cry broke the silence.

"Can it be?" he mused, frowning quizzically. "But no. Never does a woman pray alone to God in His Temple! Scarcely have I even seen a man so come to God."

The priest sat up straight, as if his thoughts demanded greater dignity of posture. Jehovah's Temple was a house of prayer, indeed! Solemn, reverent, liturgical prayer, that is. Did this woman not know that God was unapproachable, except by authorized forms of Temple worship? Was she so presumptuous as to think that she, a peasant woman, could gain the ear of a holy God?

And still, he noted, she carried on—sometimes falling on her face, sometimes gazing heavenward; now utterly silent, now sobbing softly.

No, Eli said firmly to himself, *this woman is not praying!*

The old man rose from his chair and walked toward the prostrate figure. When he stood directly over her, he said almost harshly: "How long will you remain in your drunken condition? Oh, foolish woman, put your wine away!" The woman raised her face to Eli. "No, no, sir," she said clearly. "Do not misjudge me. My heart is breaking with sorrow. I was pouring out my soul before the Lord."

Eli looked at her, strangely confused. Indeed, he thought he could trace, through her white veil, the streaks of tears on her cheeks. He could not believe that the eyes of this soft-spoken woman were glassy with alcohol.

Reaching out a time-wrinkled hand, he touched her bowed head.

"Go in peace," he told her, "and the God of Israel give to you the thing which you have so earnestly asked of Him."

The woman stood to her feet and slipped quietly out of the sanctuary. Eli shook his head as he watched her steady step.

"Was that a smile of peace I saw on her lips?" he pondered aloud. Then, seating himself once more beside a post of the Temple of God in Shiloh, he added, "If that sort of praying brings such relief, would to God more of His people would practice it."

WOMAN'S PRAYER

What is prayer?

Volumes have been written to answer this question. For prayer, like a finely cut diamond, is a many-sided treasure. In this brief study, we shall not try to uncover all its secrets. But looking at the life of Hannah, we will consider how prayer can be meaningful and rewarding for a woman.

As with the lives of Rahab and Ruth, Hannah's story begins with a problem. Read 1 Samuel 1:1-7 to discover Hannah's problem.

NOTE: In the King James Version, verse 6 speaks of Hannah's "adversary." Other translations make it clear that this refers to Peninnah, Elkanah's other wife.

1. How did Elkanah try to console her (1 Samuel 1:5-8)?

Why did he not succeed? _____

NOTE: Childlessness was considered in Bible days a sign of God's displeasure. Understandably, then, no amount of her husband's love could erase from Hannah's heart the grief of feeling rejected by God.

2. Where did Hannah go, and what did she do to find relief from her pressures (1 Samuel 1:9-10)?

_____

Read Philippians 4:6. The word "careful" in the KJV means "anxious." Note what God expects us to do with our problems.

OBSERVATION: Often God forces us, by the pressure of circumstances, into a place of desperation. If we allow these trials to press us close to Him in prayer, they will lead us to a rich, full life built on confidence in Him. If, however, we rebel and accuse God of injustice, we develop into bitter, cold, shriveled souls.

3. Read Psalm 61:1-2; 62:8; 63:1. What kind of prayer is indicated in these verses?

_____

Does this sound like Hannah? _____

OBSERVATION: When we pour out our hearts before God, we expose to Him all their contents.

4. Read Hebrews 4:14-16. Sorrows, joys, failures, doubts, successes—is there anything we need fear to bring to God?

_____

Why can we be confident of acceptance when we come to God in prayer?

_____

How will God react when we are open and honest with Him?

_____

5. Was Hannah's vow in 1 Samuel 1:11 a form of bribery or an expression of devotion? (Remember that her desire to

have a son may have been less than her yearning to be accepted by God.)

When a young man was set apart to live a life fully dedicated to God's service, he was required, by God's laws, to demonstrate this dedication by certain outward signs. Read about these in Numbers 6:1-5. Hannah promised just this kind of dedication for her son (1 Samuel 1:11).

OBSERVATION: Hannah broke the laws of custom by praying alone in the Temple (1 Samuel 1:12-16) because need had broken her heart. True prayer is essentially conversation with God. It is not limited by set forms, places, times, postures, or words.

6. Note the change in Hannah's spirit (1 Samuel 1:8, 18). What do you think caused this change? Had her circumstances changed? Had she received any concrete assurance that God would give her what she had asked?

Read 1 Samuel 1:19-20. Names often carried special meaning in Bible days—hence, the logic of Hannah's choice of name for her son. *Samuel* means "asked of God."

NOTE: Read 1 Samuel 1:19-28. Verse 24 speaks of the time when "she had weaned him." According to custom of that day, Samuel was probably about three years old at this time. Many Bible scholars believe there were women serving in the Temple who would have cared for the young boy.

7. By keeping her vow, what did Hannah prove concerning the sincerity of her prayer?

The purity of her motivation?

The stability of her character?

---

8. What special reward did God give to Hannah for her faithfulness (1 Samuel 2:19-21, 26)?

_____

How does Hannah's story illustrate the principle stated in Matthew 6:33 and Psalm 37:4-5?

_____

_____

Try to imagine how differently the story might have ended had Hannah gone back on her promise to God and kept Samuel for herself. What is the connection between prayer, obedience, and God's blessing on our lives?

_____

_____

OBSERVATION: We can never sacrifice anything precious to God, but that He gives us something far better in return.

9. Study Hannah's prayer in 1 Samuel 2:1-10. Is she asking for anything? _____

What is the main theme of her prayer? _____

What does this prayer tell us about the condition of Hannah's heart? _____

_____

10. Prayer takes many forms. Just as communication between two human beings varies to meet needs of expression, so does prayer. Read the following verses to discover some of the different kinds of prayer mentioned in Scripture:

Psalm 51; 1 John 1:9 _____

Psalm 135:1-3 _____

Matthew 6:11; Philippians 4:6 _____

Romans 8:26 _____

Ephesians 5:20 _____

1 Timothy 2:1-4 _____

11. What kinds of things do you pray about?

_____

_____

Do you feel you need to enlarge the scope of your praying?

_____

12. Whatever form our prayers may take, the important ingredient is attitude. What attitudes do the following verses tell us are needed for effective praying?

Psalm 27:14 _____

Matthew 6:5-8 _____

Matthew 7:7-8 _____

Matthew 21:22 _____

Mark 11:25 _____

Luke 18:1 _____

James 5:16 _____

GET THE POINT

Woman's prayer is the pouring out of her heart and all its contents to God, then watching Him transform her offering into some beautiful and useful work of art.

Prayer Is

Prayer is
God on His throne,
In His universe
In my kitchen,
At my elbow
All day long.

Prayer is
Sharing with God
Joy and happiness,
Pain and heartache,
Every feeling
My heart holds.

> Prayer is
>   Giving over
>   Problems so sticky,
>   God must mix them
>   With His wisdom
>   For solution.

FURTHER READING

Amplified Old Testament. Grand Rapids: Zondervan, 1964. P. 790.

Butler, J. Glentworth. *Butler's Bible Work: The Gospels.* New York: Funk & Wagnall, 1889. Sections 179, 183.

———. *Topical Analysis of the Bible.* New York: Butler Bible Work, 1897. Pp. 377, 383-6.

Douglas, J. D., ed. *The New Bible Dictionary.* Grand Rapids: Eerdman's, 1962. Pp. 504, 1019-20, 1242-3, 1340.

Hallesby, O. *Prayer.* Minneapolis: Augsburg, 1931.

Halley, Henry H. *Bible Handbook,* 22d ed. Chicago: Henry H. Halley, 1959. Pp. 170-1.

Rinker, Rosalind. *Prayer: Conversing With God.* Grand Rapids: Zondervan, 1959.

9
Jochebed

INTRODUCING JOCHEBED

Jochebed sat on a low stool in her mud hut. At her breast, a handsome baby boy sucked hungrily. She smoothed the thin curls back from his forehead. He opened his eyes, and the young mother noted a smile turning up the corners of his tiny mouth.

"Thank God you're mine, son," she whispered, and then added, "At least for a while."

"Just think how pleased Father will be to hear the good news," fifteen-year-old Miriam said from the corner of the room, where she was cooking flat cakes for the evening meal.

Jochebed thought back to that morning, when she and Miriam had slipped quietly down to the river where Pharaoh's daughter bathed. They had set their crudely pitched basket among the reeds and gently pushed it from the shore.

Jochebed had worked the rest of the morning at her grinding and cleaning, like a woman in a dream. Her heart was in that little basket down on the river. How thankful she was for Miriam's watchful eyes!

She had been so afraid. Yet surely God would understand her doubts. Times were so dreadful. And the king's latest decree, ordering the death of all Hebrew baby boys—it was unthinkable!

"If God has helped us hide our baby these three months, He will protect him today, too," Miriam had assured her mother when they first talked of the plan.

Now, still a bit awed by the way Jehovah *had* protected her son, Jochebed looked down at him. His chubby nose nestled into her breast. One little fist reached wildly toward her face. Laughing, he gurgled his thanks for a satisfying meal. Jochebed squeezed him.

"I wonder what God has planned for this baby," she mused as she placed him into the woolen cradle suspended from the roof beams. "He will go to live in the king's palace. No more poverty or ignorance, and he will never be a slave like Amram, his father."

Three-year-old Aaron came running to rock his little brother.

"Mommy," he asked, his eyes wide with wonder, "will we teach the baby about God?"

Jochebed hastily brushed a tear from her eye, with the corner of her gray shawl. "Indeed we shall! And you can help, Aaron." She walked to the kitchen area to help Miriam with the supper.

"Come! Hurry, Mommy!" Aaron called. "Baby is crying. Soldiers will find him."

The young mother smiled. "No, we don't need to keep him quiet any longer. He belongs to Pharaoh's princess now."

A happy Jochebed stood still and listened for a long moment. For the first time, the lusty cry coming from the cradle failed to trigger panic in her heart.

"Thank God," she murmured. "That sound is music to my ears!"

WOMAN'S MOTHERHOOD

Marriage and a family do not fit into God's plan for every woman. But even the woman who never gives birth to a child or adopts one, or whose children are now grown and gone, may find herself mothering someone else's children. God has given to women special faculties, peculiar sensibilities, and unique insights that make for effective mothering. Each woman's world is filled with people in need of the feminine touch—either physically, emotionally, or spiritually.

So this study is for all women. Everything we say about a

mother and her child can be applied in any mothering situation where God may place you.

Again, our subject is broad. It is impossible to focus on all the aspects of motherhood in one short lesson, so we have narrowed it down. Our plan is to establish from Scripture the ultimate goal of motherhood and to apply it to our constantly changing mothering roles.

Read about the unusual situation of the Hebrew people at the time of the birth of Jochebed's third child, Moses (Exodus 1).

OBSERVATION: Hundreds of baby boys died under this inhuman royal edict. While there may have been several survivors, God, for special reasons (which we will pick up as we progress) gives us the unusual record of only one that lived.

1. How did Jochebed try to save her endangered son (Exodus 2:1-4)?

_____

_____

According to the record in the "faith chapter" of the Bible, what motivated her to attempt this rescue (Hebrews 11:23)?

_____

2. Read Exodus 2:5-10. In an unprecedented turn of events, Jochebed cared for her son while receiving wages from a princess for doing so. This arrangement probably lasted for about three years, as that was the normal time for weaning. Since she was a woman of faith, how would you suppose she trained him spiritually during those early years?

_____

3. How much emphasis should a parent place on spiritual training in the home (see Deuteronomy 6:6-9)?

_____

Judging from scriptural example and admonition, when is the best time to begin a child's spiritual training (Proverbs 22:6; 2 Timothy 3:14-15)?

_____

_____

4. God's plan for Moses was outstanding. Read in Genesis 15:13-14 the promise He had given to Abraham about the future of his descendents, the Hebrews (here referred to as Abraham's seed). Now read Acts 7:17-22, 35-36. Where did Moses fit into the picture?

_____

Is it likely that Jochebed knew of Moses' place in God's plan when she protected him in a basket of reeds or was she simply doing her duty with strong faith in God?

_____

_____

OBSERVATION: Faith in the God who gives us our children sees the potential in each budding life. Though we cannot see the ultimate plan of God, faith tells us to spare nothing to see that all the potential is developed.

5. List some practical ways in which mothers can help their children develop their spiritual potential.

_____

_____

_____

According to 2 Timothy 3:14-17, what is the basic guidebook for effective spiritual training?

_____

Are the Scriptures relevant to all of a child's spiritual needs (see verse 16)?

_____

6. How did God use Moses' special training to prepare him for his life's work (Acts 7:21-22)?

_____

_____

Did Moses always follow God's wisdom in his attempt to fulfill divine mission (Acts 7:23-29)?

_____

7. Imagine how Jochebed must have felt if she heard of Moses' dreadful error. Remember, she did not have the promises of the Bible to comfort her when things went wrong.

What encouragement do the Scriptures give today's mothers to persevere in hope when things look bleak (1 Corinthians 15:58; Galatians 6:9; Hebrews 10:36)?

How does this apply to discouraging periods of child rearing?

8. Note the priorities Moses set for his later life (Hebrews 11:24-27). What evidence do you see in this passage that Jochebed's faith was reproduced in her son?

9. Not only was Moses' life the fruit of Jochebed's faith; her other two children, though they did not perform as prominent a task as Moses, played important roles in Israel's spiritual history. What position distinguished Aaron (Exodus 4:14-16; 28:1, 12, 38)?

Miriam (Exodus 15:20-21)? _____

OBSERVATION: Jochebed reached the goal of godly motherhood: the growth of mature sons and daughters dedicated to God, making their own way in life, and helping others along the road to Christian maturity.

10. To reach this goal, we mothers need a wisdom beyond ourselves. How can we obtain it (James 1:5)?

11. Consider the promise of Proverbs 22:6. What is meant by the word "train"? How does the child's free will enter the picture? Can we necessarily expect to see the fulfillment of this promise in our lifetime? When and how must we

take hands off and trust God to complete the mothering
process in our children?

_____

_____

_____

GET THE POINT

Woman's motherhood is both a priceless gift and a solemn responsibility from God. The goal of Christian motherhood is to guide each child to self-sustaining maturity in
Jesus Christ.

What Can I Do?

Confusion reigns!
My teenage daughter's let me down.
I'd counted so on her to prove
that Christian training in the home
prevents adolescent protest pains.

Instead she acts
as if I'd never helped her find
her way to God and happiness.
My sweet, submissive girl is gone!
O God, what can I do?

My child, be calm.
She is your daughter, true.
Before all else, though, she is mine.
Trust me to shape her life
the way I still am shaping yours.

FURTHER READING

Miller, Madeline S. and Lane, J. *Encyclopedia of Bible Life.*
    New York: Harper & Row, 1955. Chapter 11.
Overholtzer, Ruth. *The Life of Moses* (flannelgraph text).
    Grand Rapids: CEF, 1957.
Price, Eugenia. *Woman to Woman.* Grand Rapids: Zonder-
    van, 1959. Chapter 10.
Schaeffer, Edith. *Hidden Art.* Wheaton, Ill.: Tyndale, 1971.

10
Deborah

INTRODUCING DEBORAH

Childish shouts filled the early morning air in ancient Bethel.

"Let's play judge," called Jonathan.

"I get to be judge," shouted Rebekah.

"No you don't," Amos boomed out in his deepening voice. "That's a man's job."

"No sir!" Rebekah protested. "A woman can be judge. The head judge in Israel is Deborah, and she's a woman!"

"Pooh!" Amos countered. "My father says we shouldn't have a woman judging our country."

Just then a tall, matronly woman stepped into the dusty street from around the corner of a nearby house.

"It's Deborah!" Amos gasped, then ducked into the shadows.

Deborah's features were plain, bespeaking strength. But kindness sparkled in her eyes as she beckoned the children.

"Amos, Rebekah—all of you, come here. I want to tell you a story."

The children crowded closely around her, except for Amos, who lingered at a distance. The woman judge smiled as she began.

"Long years ago, God gave this country to our great grandparents. He wanted it always to be a wonderful home for us. So He told the people never to worship the idols of the other nations around them. He asked them to remember that He is the One who gave them their fine homes and lands."

"My uncle and his family have an idol in their village," offered Seth. "My mother and father say that is wrong."

"It is very wrong," Deborah agreed. "In fact, many people in Israel are worshiping idols now. This makes God so angry He often lets the other nations fight against us and win. When we finally pray to God, He calls some man to teach us to worship Him again."

"Is that what a judge is for?" asked Tamar, her curly hair peeking out from under a bright yellow shawl.

Edging back into the circle, Amos spoke up now: "Judges lead Israel to war, too; then we always win."

"And all is well until our people sin again," Deborah reminded them.

"But how come you decided to take over as judge?" Amos wanted to know.

"Oh, I didn't want to, Amos." Deborah shook her head. "God asked me to do it because there were no men who would do the job. Sometimes I'm afraid. Every day I must ask God to help me."

"Does He really do it?" Amos challenged.

"Yes, He does."

"That ought to show the old idol worshipers that Jehovah is pretty strong," Rebekah said.

"I hope and pray it will." Deborah patted the girl's head and walked away.

The children were quiet a moment. Then Rebekah spoke: "I've got an idea. Let's play it like it ought to be in Israel. Amos, you be the judge. I'll be your wife and stay in my tent and fix supper while you go out and judge the people."

WOMAN'S STRENGTH

Deborah lived in a morally corrupt society. The nation Israel, established by God to spread His knowledge to all peoples, had instead adopted the idol-worshiping ways of heathen neighbors they were to have helped. As their moral fiber deteriorated, national identity became fuzzy. Weakened by the process, they fell easily into slavery to the militarily stronger nations they had tried to imitate.

This is the study of one unusual woman whose supernatural strength of character God used to rescue Israel from extinction. We will examine her life to see the source and effectiveness of a woman's strength.

1. According to Judges 2:1-3, what was the big mistake of the people of Israel?

_____

NOTE: In the book of Judges, a cycle of apostasy (turning away from God) is repeated six times. Each complete cycle includes the following stages:

a. Sin—"the children of Israel did evil in the sight of the Lord"
b. Servitude—"The Lord delivered them into the hands of their enemies"
c. Supplication—"the children of Israel cried unto the Lord"
d. Salvation—"the Lord raised up judges which delivered them"
e. Security—"and the land had rest"
f. Sin again—"the children of Israel did evil again"

2. Who were Israel's oppressors when Deborah came on the scene (Judges 4:1-3)? List them by name:

(a) the king _____

(b) the nation _____

(c) the army general _____

How long had Israel been oppressed by these enemies (Judges 4:3)?

_____

3. Who was Deborah, and why did the people come to her for help (Judges 4:4-5)?

_____

_____

NOTE: A prophet was one who spoke the words of God. He was comparable to a preacher of today, though he usually also had special gifts for foretelling the future.

The judge was the sole political leader during this period of Israel's history. He handled matters of justice and led the military.

BACKGROUND STUDY: The Bible records only ten women who were called prophetesses. Read about them, and identify them:

Exodus 15:20 _____

Judges 4:4 _____

2 Kings 22:14 _____

Nehemiah 6:14 _____

Isaiah 8:3 _____

Luke 2:36 _____

Acts 21:8-9 _____
All were unusual women, and most of them served the Lord in times of national crisis.

4. From whom had Deborah received her orders for battle strategy (Judges 4:6-7)?

_____

OBSERVATION: As a prophetess, Deborah was one of the few people in Israel's spiritually declining society who lived close enough to God to hear His message and gain courage to speak it.

5. What kind of a man was Barak (Judges 4:8)?

_____

6. What was Deborah's actual role in the victorious battle (Judges 4:9-10)?

_____

OBSERVATION: Barak's faith was so weak he had to lean on a woman to sustain him. Often God gives to women this special ministry of upholding those whose faith is weaker. (See Galatians 6:1-2 for a statement of God's provision for strengthening weak believers.)

7. What three things did God use to defeat Sisera and his armies?

(a) Judges 4:15-16 _____

(b) Judges 4:17-22 _____

(c) Judges 5:20-21 _____

NOTE: While God may or may not have condoned Jael's method of defeating Sisera, He used her courage to accomplish Israel's deliverance.

8. To whom did Deborah give the glory for Israel's victory (Judges 5:1-3)?

_____

OBSERVATION: By relying on divine strength, Deborah brought peace to her nation. It is often characteristic of the "fairer sex" to long and strive for peace—individually, in the home, in the community, in the nation, and to the end of the world.

9. How is the condition of our nation today similar to that of Deborah's Israel? What can we women do to strengthen the weak spots in our society?

_____

_____

10. Who is our sole source of spiritual and moral strength (Ephesians 6:10)?

_____

How are we instructed to appropriate this strength (Ephesians 6:11-18)?

_____

_____

OBSERVATION: We women need strength of conviction and strength to overcome sin, to develop mature behavior, and to endure difficulties. God can equip us in all these areas.

11. What kinds of people can God use most effectively, and why (1 Corinthians 1:26-31; 2 Corinthians 12:9-10)?

_____

_____

OBSERVATION: God does not use us because of who or what we are, but because we have yielded ourselves to His power (see Romans 6:12-14). The measure of our strength is determined by our yieldedness to Him; because the only true strength we possess is His, not ours.

12. In what practical ways can you yield yourself to God today, so He can pour His power through you into the decaying society where you live?

_____

_____

GET THE POINT

Woman's strength lies in her willingness to let God do His work through her life.

True Strength

Have you not known? Have you not heard?
The LORD is a God everlasting,
The Creator of the ends of the earth.
He does not faint, nor grow weary;
His insight is unfathomable.
He gives power to the fainting,
And to him that has no might he increases strength.
Though the youths faint and grow weary,
Though the young men fall prostrate,
They that wait on the LORD shall renew their strength,
They shall mount on wings like eagles,
They shall run and not be weary,
They shall walk and not faint.[1]

ISAIAH 40:28-31

FURTHER READING

Douglas, J. D., ed. *The New Bible Dictionary*. Grand Rapids: Eerdman's, 1962. Pp. 303, 676-77.

1. Alex R. Gordon, trans., "Isaiah," in *The Complete Bible, An American Translation* (Chicago: U. of Chicago, 1939). Copyright 1939 by the University of Chicago. All rights reserved. Used by permission.

11
Samaritan Woman

INTRODUCING THE SAMARITAN WOMAN

"Come, follow me! See a man who told me all I ever did!" A woman's excited voice shattered the silence of Sychar's noon-hour streets.

Three leathery-skinned farmers lounged under an old olive tree in the city square. They lifted their eyebrows at the gaudily dressed woman.

"So what?" asked one.

"Not too pretty a story, eh?" another added, and the men guffawed.

Noisy metal bracelets jangling from her thin arms, the woman gestured pleadingly. "Even though I've never seen Him before, He knows all about me. Is not He the Christ, the promised Messiah?"

A brown-faced little toddler appeared in an open doorway nearby. In an instant his mother looked out, blinking at the sunlight. Seeing the woman, she gave a shriek, and pulled her child inside.

"Well, are you coming with me or not?" The woman stood before them, hands resting on shapely hips.

"Oh, I suppose," one man drawled, rising to his feet with mock difficulty.

"We may as well." And the other two followed his example.

"You just won't believe it until you see Him yourselves," the woman shouted, hurrying her reluctant followers through the village streets. Beckoning to other groups of idle bystanders, she repeated her pleas again and again. The strange procession left town and bustled down a dusty roadway into the ampitheatre-shaped valley between Mount Ebal and Mount Gerizim.

"Hey, lady," someone shouted. "You sure this man is really the Messiah?"

Without slowing her pace she retorted, "Would I have called you if I wasn't sure?"

The man grinned and then shouted with enthusiasm, "Just wait till this news reaches Jerusalem. The Messiah, a *Samaritan*, establishing His kingdom in *Sychar!*"

"Yeah!" There was a tremendous shout.

"And we shall reign with him," called another, evoking more loud cheers.

Suddenly the man directly behind the woman stopped. Spreading his arms wide across the path, he let his sleeves hang like curtains, holding back the others.

The woman had gone a few feet further before she noticed she was alone. Turning, she asked, "Changed your minds?"

The merchant in the lead spoke: "That man up there—those men—sitting by Jacob's well." His voice dropped to a fearful whisper. "They—they're Jews! We can't go near them. They'll spit on us!"

The woman raised her voice in defense: "Sure they're Jews. Who said they weren't? But one of them *is* the Messiah of God! I know it!"

Without hesitation, she climbed the small knoll which led to the ancient well. Her puzzled cohorts followed, the merchant shaking his head and muttering into his beard, "I just don't understand."

WOMAN'S PREJUDICE

Jesus lived in a day of open prejudice. Jews hated Samaritans, and Samaritans hated Jews. Romans ruled Jews and Samaritans and were hated by both alike. Religious leaders were jealous of one another's popularity. Rebels, defectors, and rioters filled the little Palestinian nation with unrest. Prejudices were built on ancient traditions, and blood ran hot in the veins of these Middle Eastern peoples.

Into such an explosive society Jesus stepped, with His

startling truth that God loves all alike and wants all to love each other in *His* way.

In the story of the unnamed Samaritan woman of John 4, we see Jesus' confrontation with an actual case of prejudice and His skillful, tenderly loving way of handling it.

JOHN 4:1-9—*Woman's prejudice may be very strong.*

1. Most Jews traveling from Judea to Galilee crossed to the eastern side of the Jordan River in order to avoid walking through Samaria. (Consult a map in the back of your Bible or Bible atlas, showing Palestine in Jesus' day.) Why do you think Jesus felt He had to go through Samaria (John 4:3-4)?

_____

This gives us a glimpse of the divine side of Jesus. How do verses 5-7 show us that Jesus was also truly human?

_____

NOTE: Verse 6 could be translated, in part, "Jesus, utterly exhausted from His journey, flung Himself wearily on the seat, anxious for complete solitude and rest."

2. How did Jesus startle the woman who came to the well (John 4:7-9)?

_____

NOTE: Jesus broke two strong Jewish customs that day in Samaria: (a) A Jewish man never addressed a woman in public. If he were a Rabbi, or religious teacher, he might not even speak publicly with his wife. (b) No conscientious Jew would drink from a vessel which had been "contaminated" by Samaritan hands.

3. What kinds of prejudice do we harbor?

_____

Do they always have a solid, logical basis?

_____

JOHN 4:10-15: *Woman's prejudice can lead to misunder-*

standing, both of the people against whom she is prejudiced and of the ways of God with her.

4. What did the woman not understand about Jesus (John 4:10-12)?

What did Jesus mean when He offered her living water (John 4:10-14; see also Psalm 42:1-2; John 7:37-39)?

5. How can prejudice keep us from knowing Christ personally?

JOHN 4:16-26: *Woman's prejudice must be exposed* (1) by recognizing her true self, (2) by understanding the nature of God, and (3) by discovering the person of Jesus Christ.

6. How did Jesus help the Samaritan woman recognize her true self (John 4:16-18)?

Read Proverbs 28:13. Note how necessary it is to face our sin before we can receive the life God has for us.

7. Uncomfortable at having her personal sin exposed, the woman quickly turned to another question. What kind of topic did she mention, to sidetrack Jesus from the subject that had touched a sensitive nerve with her (John 4:19-20)?

NOTE: "This mountain," in John 4:20, refers to Mount Gerizim, towering above Jesus and the woman as they talked. Many years before, King Mannaseh had built a temple on Gerizim's peak. For centuries Jews and Samaritans had argued over where was the proper place to worship God, in Jerusalem or on Mount Gerizim.

8. Instead of pursuing the argument the woman presented to Him, Jesus put His finger on the thing that makes

worship proper. How did He say worshipers must approach God (John 4:21-24)?

Now thoroughly confused, how did the woman try to dismiss the whole subject (John 4:25)?

OBSERVATION: Jews and Samaritans alike were looking for the soon coming of a Messiah, or deliverer, who would set right the evils of their society and liberate them from Roman rule. God had promised this Messiah throughout the Old Testament. Jesus came to fulfill God's promises, but differently than men expected. He came to liberate men not from political conquerors but from sin and prejudice.

9. How did Jesus further startle the woman and thus block off her last route of escape from exposure (John 4:26)?

How does Christ confront us with the problem areas of our lives?

JOHN 4:27-42: *Woman's prejudice can be overcome.*

10. Does the woman's testimony in John 4:28-29 seem to indicate that her faith in Jesus Christ had helped overcome her prejudice?

How did the breakdown of one woman's prejudice against one lone Jew affect a whole Samaritan village (John 4:39-42)?

Note the words of the villagers in verse 42: "[We] know this is indeed . . . the Saviour *of the world.*"

BACKGROUND STUDY: For additional light on Jesus' feelings about prejudice, read the story He told in Luke 10:25-37.

11. Read 1 Corinthians 13 and discover the one Christ-like virtue that provides a sure cure for prejudice.

12. How must we respond to Christ's exposure of our selves before He can liberate us?

GET THE POINT

Woman's prejudices are a hindrance to growth. She must allow Jesus Christ to destroy them so that she can find the path to personal wholeness and blessing to others.

Prejudice Is

PREJUDICE IS refusing housing to a family of a racial minority;
prejudice is also turning out a wayward son or daughter because he or she has "disgraced" the family.

PREJUDICE IS paying a worker less because she is a woman;
prejudice is also giving a child in your Sunday school class less love because he is dirty and shabbily dressed.

PREJUDICE IS not letting your son play with the boy on the corner because his skin color doesn't match yours;
prejudice is also refusing to visit your neighbor's church because it does not agree with yours on everything.

PREJUDICE IS calling a person a derogatory name because he is from another country;
prejudice is also labeling a fellow church-member "uncommitted" because she will not make room in her schedule for your project.

PREJUDICE IS omitting a poor person from your guest list;
prejudice is also refusing to invite a divorcee to your monthly circle meeting.

PREJUDICE IS insisting on pouring your child into your desired occupational mold;

prejudice is also rejecting your child's choice of marriage partner because he or she is "not good enough."

PREJUDICE IS snubbing a woman whose house is poorer than yours;
prejudice is also ignoring a woman because she has experienced mental illness and is having trouble in relationships.

PREJUDICE IS turning your back on the needs that press at your door;
prejudice is also ignoring God's plea to face your prejudice for the sin it is; to confess it; and, with His help, to forsake it.

FURTHER READING

Butler, J. Glentworth. *Topical Analysis of the Bible.* New York: Butler Bible Work, 1897. Sections 22-23.

Douglas, J. D., ed. *The New Bible Dictionary.* Grand Rapids: Eerdman's, 1962. Pp. 1130-32.

Farrar, F. W. *The Life of Christ.* London: Cassell, n.d. Chapter 15.

Ingles, James Wesley. *A Woman of Samaria.* Grand Rapids: Zondervan, 1972.

Lovelace, Delos W. *Journey to Bethlehem.* New York: Crowell, 1953. Chapters 7-9.

Price, Eugenia. *Beloved World.* Grand Rapids: Zondervan, 1961. Chapter 29.

12
Dorcas, Lydia, and Priscilla

INTRODUCING DORCAS, LYDIA, AND PRISCILLA

A full moon peered out from behind the massive peak of Acro-Corinth. As the huge, glowing ball rose higher in a cloud-strewn sky, its golden light flowed down the steep sides of the mountain, where the temple of Apollo glistened in its rays. Then it shed a romantic luminescence over Corinth, spread out on the plain below.

The magnificent buildings of this wealthy capital city of southern Greece rose out of a tangled mass of wretched, wood-and-straw huts.

In one of these huts, Aquila the tentmaker sat at his roughly-hewed table with his wife, Priscilla, and business partner, Paul. Neatly tied bundles leaned against the mud-daubed walls. One tiny, clay lamp resting on the table sent elusive shadows prancing about the barren room.

"We have spent many pleasant hours together here," Aquila said, "but seldom has the house been so quiet." He chuckled.

"I shall remember it as it has most often been—filled with people," Priscilla said wistfully.

"Filled with new Christians," Paul corrected. "Even in this sin-loving, pagan city. It is a true miracle!"

Priscilla tapped a graceful finger pensively on the table. "As we leave Corinth and go on to begin a new church in Ephesus, Paul, one thing disturbs me." Her brow tightened into worried little furrows. "I want to serve my Lord well, but properly. When I think of service, I remember Dorcas. Like the virtuous woman in Solomon's writings, she sewed and cooked for the poor widows and orphans of Joppa. But, tell me, is this the only acceptable way for a woman to serve Jesus?"

Paul spoke with his characteristic authority: "In Philippi lived a wealthy merchant-woman named Lydia. We led her to Christ, and she opened her home to meet our needs. She also witnessed daily to her business associates of her faith in Christ."

Priscilla sighed. "To open my home, to witness to my friends and neighbors—yes, I know these services please God. But I long to have a more direct part in the growth of new churches."

Twisting a short length of tent cord, she went on. "I fear it's wrong, for I'm only a woman. But my heart is so full of good things from the Lord, and—well—I feel I must teach some of the new converts."

Aquila smiled at his wife. "My heart is no less full than yours. But, my dear Prisca, I could never find words to express myself as you can."

The lamp flickered and desperate flames shot out. Thin, diehard shadows leaped at Paul's face as he said, "To one God gives the gift of expressive speech and the strong urge to use that gift; to another, the deeper ministry of prevailing prayer. Is He mistaken if He gives the more noticeable gift to a man's wife?"

Priscilla took the now darkened lamp in her hands and let the light of the moon, filtering through a tiny window, fall full upon it.

"Then perhaps," she mused, "this love to teach is God's lamp in my hands—to keep burning for Him."

Paul added, "Only take care that you let Him control its fuel and flame."

Aquila slipped a strong arm around his wife and drew her back to the seat beside him, and the three church workers bowed their heads to pray.

WOMAN'S SERVICE

In Bible times, women were looked upon as second-class

citizens. Thinking themselves superior in every way, men had twisted God's commandments and were using them as an occasion for holding women in slavelike subjection.

Mary, the mother of Jesus, put a lie to their claim and began to lift the status of womankind. Conceiving a son without the aid of a man, she proved that women, too, could relate directly with God and carry out a divine mission.

In this lesson we will trace God's pattern of service for Christian women as it developed in the early Church. Three women mentioned in the book of Acts demonstrate for us three different types of service acceptable to God.

DORCAS—HELPING THE NEEDY
Read Acts 9:36-42.
1. To what had Dorcas dedicated her life (Acts 9:36)?

_____

OBSERVATION: First-century Hebrews were quite family oriented. The sort of thing for which Dorcas was so much loved in her city was nearly unheard-of outside of the family. One outstanding mark of the Christian Church, however, was its social concern. Hence, such works of charity were uncommon everywhere except among Christian women of that day. To Dorcas, such service was the natural expression of a compassionate heart. It was the dedication of her domestic talents to God on behalf of others.

2. Specifically, what kind of things did her service include (Acts 9:39)?

_____

Do you think her ministry may have included such other things as distributing food, caring for children, and tending the sick?

_____

NOTE: Dorcas lived in Joppa, the main seaport serving Jerusalem. Such a community of seagoing people would be apt to have a great many widows and orphans. Opportunities for Dorcas to minister in the name of Jesus Christ were probably numberless.

3. What is the social-service obligation of today's Christian woman (James 1:27; 2:15-16; 1 John 3:16-18)?

_____

_____

4. According to Jesus' familiar words in Matthew 25:34-40, what are we really doing when we help our fellowman in need?

_____

OBSERVATION: To you, sewing a garment, baking a casserole, chauffeuring a woman to the doctor, or watching a child while his mother works to support her family may all seem insignificant, mundane deeds. Perhaps you always do these kinds of things and yet feel you have no special talents to use for the Lord. Dorcas is in the Bible to say to you: Whatever the deed, if it is done for Him in love, it is a special service (see Matthew 10:42).

Remember, Dorcas, who never led a choir, taught a Sunday school class, or ran the women's missionary society, was the only woman in the New Testament to be called a disciple (Acts 9:36)!

5. List some practical ways that you personally might (or already do) involve yourself in meeting physical and material needs of others.

_____

_____

_____

LYDIA—SHARING HER HOME

Read Acts 16:9-15, 40. (Note: Macedonia was one of the provinces of Greece.)

Lydia was one of the few career women in the New Testament. An industrious businesswoman, she came from Thyatira, an important center of trade and manufacturing.

Probably she worked as overseas agent of a large textile manufacturer (perhaps a wealthy family business).

6. Lydia became the first recorded convert to Christianity in Europe. How did she use her hospitality as a service to the Lord (Acts 16:14-15, 40)?

OBSERVATION: Philippians 1:5 and 4:10, 15 seem to imply that hospitality, as a Christian service and means of spreading the Gospel, became a traditional feature of the church in Philippi. We cannot help wondering how much Lydia's influence had to do with this.

7. Christian service has little value to God unless it is properly motivated. According to 1 Peter 4:7-11, what one motive is needed to make hospitality, or any other Christian service, acceptable (see also 1 Corinthians 13:1-3)?

What will be our attitude if we serve with proper motives (Psalm 100:2; Colossians 3:23)?

8. How can hospitality be a service to the Lord today?

To whom should we extend hospitality (Luke 14:12-14; Galatians 6:10; Hebrews 13:2)?

PRISCILLA—INSTRUCTING NEW BELIEVERS

Read Acts 17:33—18:3, 24-28; Romans 16:3-5.

9. How did Priscilla use what she had learned from Paul to help train a young minister (Acts 17:33—18:3, 24-28)?

OBSERVATION: In a day when women were discouraged from developing their intellectual abilities, Priscilla dared to use hers; but she let Jesus Christ control them. Priscilla and Aquila were an unusual husband-and-wife team, working together in the churches. Some Bible scholars believe Priscilla was the more aggressive partner, partly because, in a couple of places, Paul mentions her name before Aquila's—an unheard-of form of address in New Testament times.

10. In what ways did Priscilla and Aquila serve the Lord together (Romans 16:3-5)?

NOTE: In the earliest times, church groups met in private homes, not in recognized buildings. Often those who opened their homes also led the group.

11. Once we have trusted Christ, to whom do we belong—body, soul, possessions, and ambitions (1 Corinthians 6:19-20)?

For what, then, does God hold us responsible (Romans 12:1-2)?

How should we feel if we cannot do the job someone else does so well? Is one job more important than another (Romans 12:3-8)?

---

12. Romans 12:1-2 is a plea for dedication of our total being to Jesus Christ. The remainder of Romans 12 and all of Romans 13 present practical ways of working out this dedication. For example, the practice of hospitality is mentioned in 12:13. Study Romans 12 and 13 with pencil and paper, jotting down the different ways suggested that you can serve the Lord.

GET THE POINT

Woman's service is to love Jesus Christ and make herself available to help meet others' needs as He directs.

Please Let Me Be Me

Please let me be me, Friend.
  God lets me;
    why can't you?

Last year you pushed me, pushed me hard.
  Said God had given you a great program,
    and I was the key to its success.

I hesitated,
  knowing myself—my strengths, my talents.
  My schedule was already full.

"Please let me pray about it," I said.
  "It's not good to go on impulse;
    I must ask first."

"No need," you said. "Full plans are laid—
  I'll show you every move."
    I tried to reason, but you had the answers—
    they were all so spiritual, too.

God would solve my problems, you said,
  and give me strength to do "His work."
  To that I yielded, no complaint.

I knew well that you, not God,
    had set me to the task.
  I gave God your arguments.
    But He was not convinced!

I worked too hard, I pushed myself,
  knowing God never pushes—only leads.
    In my heart bitterness grew—against you, Friend.

The price I paid last year was high:
  Drained strength, destroyed nerves,
    lost fellowship with God—
      spiritual bankruptcy.

No, Friend, I can't do your thing this year.
  Instead I pray you'll find
    you dare not push God's dear ones so—
      it's our undoing.

In fact,
   I'd like to tell you, your own schedule's too full now.
   A calmer path is more rewarding:
      God's will for you.

But God tells me to let you be you, Friend.
   He lets you,
      So I must, too.[1]

FURTHER READING

Douglas, J. D., ed. *The New Bible Dictionary.* Grand Rapids: Eerdman's, 1962. Pp. 51, 322, 760.

Farrar, F. W. *The Life and Work of Saint Paul.* London: Cassell, 1883. Chapters 24, 27-28, 31-32.

Price, Eugenia. *God Speaks to Women Today.* Grand Rapids: Zondervan, 1964. Chapters 22-24.

Redpath, Alan. *The Royal Route to Heaven.* Westwood, N.J.: Revell, 1960.

1. Ethel Herr, "Please Let Me Be Me," *Today*, Feb. 10, 1974. Used by permission of Harvest Publications.

13
Mary of Bethany

INTRODUCING MARY OF BETHANY

When Simon the leper gave a dinner for Jesus, no one was surprised that Martha insisted on cooking the meal. In fact, if she had not, Mary would have suspected her older sister was not feeling well.

"You were born to wear an apron and direct servants," Mary had told Martha when she had first learned of the affair.

Martha had smiled with pleasure at the compliment and had adjusted her linen towel to hang in precise little folds from her waistline.

On the special evening, when Simon's impressive house was filled with guests, Mary sat dreamy-eyed on a brightly colored mat near Jesus' couch. She scarcely noticed the graceful servants moving in and out between reclining couches, balancing trays of Martha's tempting foods high above their heads.

Mary was totally absorbed with Jesus—listening to His words, looking at His kind eyes, worshiping Him devotedly. Tonight she wondered dubiously about His future. It was common knowledge that since He had raised her brother Lazarus from death, His enemies, the priests in Jerusalem, had been out for His life.

I don't understand, she thought, running slender fingers through the folds of her veil flowing around her knees. *I simply can't imagine that the One who raised my dead brother to life could ever Himself be defeated by death. But I feel a strange uneasiness about Him.* She looked hard into His eyes and felt sure she saw sadness there.

Then she remembered her plan. Sudden excitement surged through her body. She straightened and felt her heart pounding very hard in her breast. Reaching out one damp hand to the polished floor beside her mat, she grasped a gray-and-white marble bottle by its slender throat. She caressed the bottle and bowed her head.

So long I've planned and waited for this moment, she mused. *I only wish my dear mother could have known the Master, too. She would have loved Him as I do. How glad I am she gave this precious gift to me before she died!*

Mary stood to her feet and walked toward Jesus. *How like a king He looks,* she said to herself. She twisted the seal on the bottle until the top came off in her hand. The penetrating aroma was delightful.

Standing behind her Master, Mary tipped the bottle and let its expensive oil trickle out onto His head. With growing enthusiasm, she moved to His feet and slowly, determinedly poured out the rest of the oil. Great drops of the ointment fell from His toes. Quickly she knelt and wiped the dripping perfume with the free-hanging tresses of her long, silken hair.

Raising her head slightly, she glanced upward. Through the corner of a misty eye, she caught a glimpse of Martha, hand on her hip, mouth round with surprise, neat head shaking in wonderment.

But when she looked at Jesus, she saw that He was smiling. Every trace of sadness had vanished from His eyes, she noted.

"*Yea, He is altogether lovely.*"[1] Mary ran the old familiar words of Scripture through her mind. With great effort she restrained herself from shouting out:

"*This is my beloved, and this is my friend, O daughters of Jerusalem.*"[2] *Come, worship Him with me!*

1. Song of Solomon 5:16.
2. Ibid.

WOMAN'S WORSHIP

Worship is
Quietly hearing God speak,
Holy hour alone with Him,
Sharing myself with Jesus Christ,
Act of love poured out on God.

Nowhere in the Bible has God given us a better example of worship than in the three pictures of Mary of Bethany. Studied side by side with her busy sister Martha, she leads us to the highest pinnacle of woman's relationships—the point of total, self-giving worship of her Creator, Saviour, Friend.

Read Luke 10:38-42.

1. As "woman of the house," what perfectly normal role did Martha play in making her guests comfortable (vv. 38, 40)?

_____

_____

Mary ignored the custom of the day which would bar her, a woman, from sitting to talk with male guests. Her love was too strong for such restrictions. Understandably, Martha was irritated by Mary's apparent laziness (vv. 39-40).

2. What was Jesus' evaluation of this "unfair" domestic situation (vv. 41-42)?

_____

_____

OBSERVATION: Often we must choose between the thing we would like to do for God and the thing He wants us to do for Him. Our choice will demonstrate the degree of our dedicated devotion (see John 14:15, 21).

3. Notice Jesus' words in Mark 10:45. His desire was to meet people's deepest spiritual needs by feeding their souls for growth. What did He want more from Martha—a sumptuous feast, or bread and cheese with time for fellowship?

_____

_____

Read John 11:1-45.

4. How did Martha act when Jesus came to raise her brother, Lazarus, from the dead (vv. 20-27, 39)?

_____

_____

What kind of instruction did Jesus give her, to calm her anxious spirit (vv. 23-26, 40)?

_____

_____

OBSERVATION: Martha, in her distracted bustle of service, had not taken time to get acquainted with her Lord. Because she had not yet been taught the truths about life and death and how Jesus was related to them, she was unprepared when the crisis came. Jesus took time to instruct her only when she was finally ready to listen. This is God's way with His children. He never forces His truth on us.

5. What does the Lord sometimes have to do in our lives to make us willing to listen to Him?

_____

6. In contrast to Martha, what single sentence did Mary offer to Jesus (v. 32)?

_____

_____

How did He react to her grief (vv. 33-35)?

_____

7. Can you see any connection between Mary's hours of worshipful learning at Jesus' feet (Luke 10) and her quiet attitude in the hour of trouble at her brother's tomb?

_____

OBSERVATION: Fellowship with God always helps us better understand divine purpose and fosters a deeper trust in the Lord in the things we cannot understand (Philippians 4:6-7).

Read John 12:1-8.

8. Devoted, visionary Mary showed her love for Jesus in what extravagant way (John 12:3)?

_____

Could Mary actually have served Jesus better by following Judas's advice? _____

Why did Jesus commend her actions (vv. 4-8)?

_____

According to verse 8, what did He imply He expected her to do in days to come, after He was gone?

_____

OBSERVATION: Wholehearted worship guides us into acceptable service. Loving service is a natural outgrowth of true worship. Love that does not express itself in service is not love. Service that does not grow out of love is service not to God but to the ego (see 1 Corinthians 13:1-3).

9. How did Mary's act benefit others?

_____

Jesus? _____

Herself? _____

OBSERVATION: Mary's deed had two lovely side effects. She filled the whole room with the sweetness of her gift, and she carried away the fragrance of her love in her hair.

10. What great distinction did Mary enjoy because of her service to Jesus (Mark 14:9)?

_____

What does this indicate about the importance of extravagant acts of worship?

_____

11. Is a woman's worship today to be confined to formal church services and structured times of family devotion? How can a woman worship Jesus Christ as an integral part of daily living (Psalm 4:4; 5:1-3; 63:1-6; John 4:23-24)?

_____

_____

94

12. Consider some practical ways you can make time in your busy schedule to talk intimately with Jesus Christ, study His Word, and worship Him. How can you express your devotion to Him practically?

_____

Extravagantly? _____

Worship is
   Recognition of Christ's presence;
   Committing every mood to Him;
   Total honesty with Heaven's King;
   Saying, "God, I love You,"
      Then trusting Him to make it fully so.

GET THE POINT

Woman's worship must be directed toward her Christ and express itself in quiet, fervent, even extravagant ways. Though sometimes misunderstood by others, such worship will one day be rewarded by Him.

Worship Acts

Mary knew You, Lord.
   Trusting, she received Your words;
   Hers was a simple,
      unencumbered faith.

Mary loved You, Lord.
   Her heart searched out a way
   to shower all the tenderness it held
      on You!

Mary performed a service
   that was special,
   costly, sweet, and beautiful.
      She gave You an experience:
         to her, a willing sacrifice;
         to You, a Father's joy.

Mary's love gift
   was spikenard in an alabaster jar.

What lavish treasure lies
protected in my closet, Lord,
that I can pour on You today?

FURTHER READING

Butler, J. Glentworth. *Butler's Bible Work: The Gospels.* New York: Funk & Wagnall, 1889. Section 90.

Chambers, Oswald. *My Utmost For His Highest.* New York: Dodd, Mead, 1952. February 21 reading.

Douglas, J. D., ed. *The New Bible Dictionary.* Grand Rapids: Eerdman's, 1962. Pp. 632, 1210.

Farrar, F. W. *The Life of Christ.* London: Cassell, n.d. Chapter 48.

Nursery Teacher. Curriculum guide for July-September 1968. Wheaton, Ill.: Scripture Press, 1968.

Price, Eugenia. *God Speaks To Women Today.* Grand Rapids: Zondervan, 1964. Chapter 18.

Moody Press, a ministry of the Moody Bible Institute, is designed for education, evangelization and edification. If we may assist you in knowing more about Christ and the Christian life, please write us without obligation to: Moody Press, c/o MLM, Chicago, Illinois 60610.